ESSAYS ON WORLD
RELIGIOUS THOUGHTS

ESSAYS ON WORLD RELIGIOUS THOUGHTS

A COMPARATIVE STUDY

◊ Hinduism
◊ Buddhism
◊ Christianity
◊ Islam
◊ African Traditional Religion
◊ Mythology
◊ Philosophy of Religion

Hyacinth Kalu

iUniverse, Inc.
Bloomington

ESSAYS ON WORLD RELIGIOUS THOUGHTS
A COMPARATIVE STUDY

iUniverse books may be ordered through booksellers or by contacting:

iUniverse
1663 Liberty Drive
Bloomington, IN 47403
www.iuniverse.com
1-800-Authors (1-800-288-4677)

ISBN: 978-1-4620-2674-6 (pbk)
ISBN: 978-1-4620-2675-3 (ebk)

Library of Congress Control Number: 2011909093

Printed in the United States of America

iUniverse rev. date:06/03/2011

THIS BOOK IS DEDIDATED TO THE INTERNATIONAL BUDDHIST EDUCATION FOUNDATION (IBEF).

TABLE OF CONTENT

CHAPTER THREE
ESSAYS ON CHRISTIANITY

CHAPTER FOUR
ESSAYS ON ISLAM

CHAPTER FIVE
ESSAYS ON AFRICAN TRADITIONAL RELIGION (ATR)

CHAPTER SIX
ESSAYS ON MYTHOLOGY

CHAPTER SEVEN
ESSAYS ON PHILOSOPHY OF RELIGION

INTRODUCTION.

Scholars and adherents of religion have differing understanding of what religion stands for, and what constitutes the meaning and purpose of religion. In their understanding of religion, some describe religion as an all-pervasive phenomenon. In this context, humans are conceived as religious animals with a yearning for worship and surrender to powers beyond them. Others see religion as a social institution like every other institution in the society. There are those who see religion as systems of belief and practice, while some see it as a soothing balm that calms the nerves of the oppressed and deprived in the society. Many more see it as an instrument and channel of inner awakening as well as connection with the divine, the ultimate reality, and or God. They are those also who think that religion was once useful, at least before the era of enlightenment and the industrial revolution, but has become obsolete in the contemporary society where the sciences seem to provide solutions to problems and questions that were hitherto referred to religion.

Among scholars and religious people, there is the problem of religious truth. What constitutes a true doctrine, which religion has the truth or the message that guarantees salvation, liberation or enlightenment? As there are differing understandings regarding the meaning and essence of religion so there are on what constitute religious truth and where we can find such truth or truths. Some religions and their followers adopt an exclusive attitude that sees their own religion as the only deposit of truth. Some adopt an inclusive attitude that acknowledges some rays of truth in other religions other than theirs. However, such truths found in other religions are considered imperfect when compared to one's own religion. There are those who adopt a more open-mind attitude on the question of religious truths. Such religions and adherents acknowledge that in all religions there are viable truths, and that all religions are expressing the truth, though in different ways. They acknowledge that it is whorth-while listening to followers of other religions with a view of understanding them and, if need be, learning from them.

I belong to this last group of scholars and adherents who believe that religious truths are not the property or priviledge of any particular religion. It is with this belief that this book is written.

This book is a collection of essays on religious thoughts across different religious traditions and belief systems in the world. It covers essays on Hinduism, Buddhism, Christianity, Islam, African Traditional Religion, Mythology, and Philosophical topics and questions on these religions. This book is not a doctrinal or historical handbook on these religions; rather it is a comparative study of these religions in terms what there are in themselves and what they have in connection with other belief systems. Again, it does not cover every minute details of comparative analysis in these religions, rather it is a collection of essays on some key issues that require clarifications and understanding within a particular religion and how they relate to other religion(s). In the treatment of the essays on each religion, brief historical facts are provided only as a clue into the religions and not an exhaustive discussion on their origins, history, beliefs and other such details.

The essays in this book are grouped into seven chapters. Chapter one presents essays on Hinduism. Chapter two is on Buddhism, while chapter three is on Christianity. Chapters four and five treat essays on Islam and African Traditional Religions, respectively. Chapters six and seven are not on any particular religion, rather they are essays across religious lines. Chapter six is on mythology. It discusses the essence of myth and how it touches on religion. Chapter seven treats philosophical issues that bear on religious interpretations, criticisms as well as the connection between religion and science. Finally, comes the evaluation and conclusion. It should be emphasized that the treatment of any particular religion in this book is not done in isolation for other religion(s); it is treated comparatively.

CHAPTER ONE

ESSAYS ON HINDUISM.

1.1 HINDUISM: BRIEF HISTORICAL FACTS.

Hinduism is oldest major religion still practiced in the world today. It predates recorded history, tracing its earliest manifestations back to the Pre-Aryan culture. What we know today as Hindu religion is a synthesis and harmonization of ancient rituals, cultures and religions. Hinduism is a polytheistic religion, believing in many gods and goddesses. Prominent among the gods are Brahma, Shiva, and Vishnu.

As a religion, Hinduism originated in India. It has no one founder. It derives its doctrines, devotions, and practices from multiple sacred texts, with the Vedas, the Upanishads, and the Bhagavad-Gita as the most revered texts. It is the third largest religion in the world today, with an estimated population of 762 million adherents.[1]

1.2 THE IMPACT OF THE PRE-ARYAN AND ARYAN CULTURES ON THE HINDU RELIGIOUS TRADITION. (A COMPARATIVE STUDY ON THE INFLUENCE OF CULTURE ON RELIGION)

Introduction

An academic study and understanding of the rich traditions of Hinduism should necessary look back to the culture that produced it – the Pre-Aryan culture. This holds true of every religious system; be it Judaism, Confucianism, Buddhism, Christianity, Islam, etc. Every religion is born within a cultural context, and as such, there is always an influence of culture on religion. What metamorphosed into a religion was first an expression of culture, a way of the people's life. To support this, Wilfred Cantwell Smith said:

> First let us note the noncivilizational people of the world: those who in their small communities and with their nonliterary traditions have provided the source material for the many informative studies of what used to be called primitive religion . . . Yet none, apparently, has traditionally had a name for that system. Nor have these groups a term for religion in general. *The persons concerned will say,* 'It is our custom [culture] to . . . ,'[1]

Granted, as we have seen, that religion is influenced by culture, the question that comes to mind is: Does culture remain the same after affecting religion? No, it does not. We can therefore, following Geertz's idea, describe culture (at least primitive, ancient, and medieval, if not modern culture) as a religious system. That is to say through the centuries, religion has also exercised tremendous influence on culture. They both impact each other positively as well as negatively.

However, our concern in this paper is to study to impact of the pre-Aryan and Aryan culture on the Hindu religious tradition. While focusing on Hinduism, we shall comparatively be drawing examples from the relationship between culture and other religions. To put our study in its proper perspective, we shall begin by attempting a general definition of culture and how it relates with religion.

Culture: A Definition

The term culture has been variously defined and understood by many scholars each from the viewpoint of his or her own field of scholarship. Etymologically, the term culture is derived:

> From the Latin *colere* meaning 'to till or cultivate'. The term is sometimes used to include all of the creative expressions of man in all fields of human endeavor. At other times, it is confined to creative expression in the areas of the liberal arts. In the second of these senses the term is sometimes extended to personal cultivation.[2]

It is generally believed that culture is the way a particular people behave, act and live. In other words, it is a way of life. It is humans that define culture, without humans there is no culture. Expressed in another way, culture is the totality of patterns according to which human beings think, act and feel. People view the whole of their experience through culture. Accordingly, Niebuhr said,

> Culture is the work of men's minds and hands. It is that portion of man's heritage in any place and time, which has been given us designedly, and laboriously by other men, not what has come to us via the mediation of nonhuman beings.[3]

Here, there is an anthropological distinction between nature and culture. Nature is what is inborn in humanity. Culture is what is nurtured in humanity through successive generations.

One of the most celebrated definitions of culture is that given by the renowned sociologist, Edward Tylor. He defined culture as "that complex whole which includes knowledge, belief, art, morals, laws customs and any other capabilities and habits acquired by man as a member of society."[4] It is clear from the definition that culture evolves and thrives within the society. Society creates culture and culture on the other hand shapes society. Culture has a social character. It is not an individual thing. Individuals experience and transmit culture uniquely, but culture transcends individual experiences. Individuals within a culture share an interactive, learned perspective on appropriate social behavior. Here culture includes the behavioral pattern of individuals within the society. In the words of Niebuhr:

> Individuals may use culture in their own ways; they may change elements in their culture, yet what they use and change is social. Culture is the social heritage they (individuals within society) receive and transmit. Whatever is purely private, so that it neither derives from nor enters into social life is not a part of culture. Conversely, social life is always cultural.[5]

Individual identity, therefore, is a by-product of cultural experience. Based on this understanding, Niebuhr, went ahead to define culture as that which "includes speech, education, tradition, myth, science, art, philosophy, government, law, rite, belief, inventions, technologies."[6]

As a people's way of life, culture, therefore, "Explicitly and implicitly teaches its members how to organize their experience. To learn a culture is to learn how to perceive, judge, and act in ways that are recognizable, predictable, and understandable to others in the same community."[7] Culture is not simply about behavior. It is also about ideas and worldviews. The mental basis of culture is commonly stressed in modern definitions of culture. For example, Clifford Geertz defines culture as, "A system of inherited conceptions expressed in symbolic forms by means of which human beings communicate, perpetuate and develop their knowledge about, and their attitudes towards life."[8]

In traditional societies, there is a very close connection between religion and culture. In his attempt to portray the connection between religion and culture and how these affect each other, Aylward Shorter said:

> Culture is essentially a transmitted pattern of meanings embodied in symbols, a pattern capable of development and change, and it belongs to the concept of humanness itself. It follows that, if religion is a human phenomenon or human activity, it must affect, and be affected by, culture.[9]

Religion can therefore be seen as part of a cultural system, and cannot exist independently or outside of culture. Culture is the vehicle for the transmission of religion, and vice versa.

The Marriage of Culture and Religion

How does culture relate to religion, or put in another way, does culture and religion generally influence each other? Yes. According to Hopfe and Woodward,

> For each religion, four major points are considered. (1) What culture produced this religion? (2) If there was a founder, and anything can be known of the founder's life, what factor caused this person to found this religion? (3) If there are scriptures or sacred texts, what do they tell us about this religion? (4) What have been the major historical developments of this religion?[10]

All these points revolve to show the interaction between culture and religion. The socio-cultural background of a religion will influence the message and choice of words in its sacred text. Its historical developments are also seen along the line of cultural epochs of the society. Taking Christianity and Jesus as an example, Jesus was born within the context of a particular culture, he grew within this culture, and he expressed and communicated his message within the cultural milieu. Put in the words of Shorter,

There could have been no earthly ministry for Jesus if he had not adopted the cultural concepts, symbols and behavior of his hearers. His cultural solidarity with the Palestinian communities of his day was a necessary condition for communicating with them.[11]

As we cannot understand Jesus and his message or religion outside the cultural context of Palestine, so we cannot understand the Hindu religious tradition outside the cultures of the pre-Aryan (Great Indus Valley civilization) and Aryan cultures.

Culture as we have already seen is the totality of a people's way of life, their ethos and world. We cannot imagine any religion coming up or taking root in any given society outside this precept. According to Geertz:

> In religious belief and practice a group's ethos is rendered intellectually reasonable by being shown to represent a way of life ideally adapted to the actual state of affair the world view describes . . . religious rituals, no matter how apparently automatic or conventional, involves the symbolic fusion of ethos and world view.[12]

In traditional societies, a clear-cut distinction between religion and culture did not so much exist. Cultural performances were also religious celebrations. In sum, culture produces religion and at the same time, culture is reshaped and understood from the religious perspective.

The Impact of the Pre-Aryan and Aryan Cultures on the Hindu Religious Tradition.

Much of what we know of the Hindu religious tradition goes back to the pre-Aryan and Aryan culture. These cultural impacts are seen both in the general Hindu religious life and in the particular practice of the some of sects in Hinduism. I use the word sects here to refer to devotees of different gods and goddesses in Hinduism, for lack of better expression. Some scholars have presented the origin of the Hindu tradition as beginning with the Aryan invasion and culture, which gave birth to the Vedic and Brahmanical traditions. Nevertheless, the origin of the Hindu religious tradition goes beyond the Aryan invasion and culture to the Indus Valley civilization centered on the cities of Harappa and Mohenjodaro. As noted by Parrinder, "Before the Aryan invasions India had possessed the most widely dispersed urban civilization the world had yet known, the Indus Valley civilization, lasting a good five hundred years from about 2300 to 1800."[13] This goes to show that:

> The Aryan did not enter a cultural vacuum. Cultural patterns nurtured in the Indus cities survived long after the cities themselves were gone. Persevered in continuing village cultures, carried southward into the Ganges Valley by late extension of the Indus civilization, maintained in the traditions of a conquered non-Aryan population, they gradually merged with Aryan culture in a great and growing synthesis.[14]

As Hopkins rightly observed, even the Aryan culture that left a lasting influence was itself influenced by earlier cultures of the Indus Valley. To used the words of Hopkins in proving this point:

> Outside religious influences on the Aryans came mostly from the primitive tradition in which magic and myth were important elements. The Aryan response was first to ignore these traditions, then gradually [began] to adopt elements that could be accommodated into the Aryan religious system. The result was a high culture fundamentally Aryan in structure but with many local and non-local Aryan beliefs and practices within it. It could expand at many levels, either by more refined intellectual development or by appropriating more popular and primitive elements. Many such expansions can be seen in the transition from early Aryan religion to the later Hindu tradition.[17]

Articulating the influence of the pre-Aryan culture on what later became Hinduism, Ainslie T. Embree wrote:

> Many aspects of later Hinduism – the god Shiva, for example – appear to have had prototypes in the Indus Valley civilization. Another source of cultural heritage was the widely scattered peoples who spoke Dravidian languages, the modern representatives of which are Tamil and Telugu. It is possible that these peoples were closely related, either ethnically or in terms of cultural influence, with the Indus Valley civilization. Probably such features of popular Hinduism as zoomorphic deities, the use of animals symbolize the supernatural, were Dravidian in origin, as may have been such important concepts of Indian thought as the belief in transmigration.[16]

Pushing the point further, Hopfe and Woodward observed that many of the statues of the pre-Aryan gods and goddess discovered by archeologists sat in lotus position; a position that was adopted by Yoga Hinduism and other meditative sect.[17] Again, the *lingam* as a symbol of male power associated with Shiva in Hinduism, and the emergence of Hindu female deities are traceable back to the pre-Aryan cultures. According to Hopkins:

> Indus religious interest seem, in summary, to have revolved around the worship of male animals raised to sacred status, the parallel worship of horned male figure represented as the Lord of (male) Creatures, worship of the *lingam* as the supreme symbol of male powers, an a conservative emphasis on order restraint, and purification by bathing, worship of the female powers of fertility and fecundity may have constituted a subsidiary cult at the popular and domestic level.[18]

All these attributes and characteristics outline by Hopkins are manifest in today's Hindu religious tradition. Furthermore, A.L. Basham rightly noted that:

> The final form of Hinduism was largely the result of the influence from the Dravidian South. Here, on the basis of the indigenous cult fertilized by Aryan influences, theistic schools had arisen, characterized by intense piety. It was this devotional Hinduism, propagated by many wandering preachers and hymn-singers in the medieval period, which had the greatest effect on Hinduism.[19]

Although the Aryan culture was not the only influence that influenced Hindu religious tradition, "The history of Hinduism begins properly with the migration waves of Aryan people into India during the second millennium B.C.E. The religion that the Aryans brought with mingled with the religion with the religion of the native people, and the culture that developed between them became classical Hinduism."[20] Let us at this point take a closer look at the particular areas of the Hindu religious traditions that bear overwhelming influences of the Aryan culture.

The Caste System: The pre-Aryan Indian society and culture knew nothing of the caste system that later became a determining factor in the Hindu religious and social life. The Aryans introduced the caste system, and this influenced and controlled Hinduism until at least the 20th century. As articulated by Basham, "The four *varnas* India developed out of very early Aryan class division, for some class stratification existed in many Indo-European communities."[21] This class division was more of a social thing in the Aryan culture but was developed into a religious framework during the Vedic tradition, with the Brahmins as the custodians of rituals and scarifies. According to Hopfe and Woodward:

> According to early sources, Aryan society began to develop into three basic classes called *varnas*. The highly regarded priests who served the cults of the various Aryan cities

were called Brahmins. The chieftains and the warriors, also considered to be near the apex of society, were called Kshatriyas. The commoners and merchants regarded as being subservient to the two upper classes were called Vaishyas. A fourth group that may have been made up of those conquered pre-Aryan people were called Shudras. Shudras were not considered full members of the society and generally held the position of slaves or servants to the Aryans. These divisions were maintained in India society for centuries and were later subdivided into the multiple classes that became the basis of the caste system [in Hindu religious life and culture.][22]

Sacrifice: Another impact of the Aryan culture on Hinduism is seen on the area of sacrifice. Sacrifice was the chief manner of worship by the Aryans. This sacrifice centered on the sacred fire—Agni, who was both priest and god. In Hindu homes and temples we still find the place and importance of fire and sacrifice. Commenting on this influence, Basham wrote, "The center of the Aryan cult was sacrifice. The cult of the domestic hearth existed in many ancient Indo-European communities, and small domestic sacrifices, performed by the head of house, must have been as important in the days of the Rig Veda as they were in Hinduism."[23]

Family Life: The family life of the Aryan was patriarchal. This patriarchal family life left its impact on the religion and family of Hinduism until recently, if at all it has changed. According to Basham, "The basic unit of Aryan society was the family. The family was staunchly patrilinear and patriarchal. The wife, though she enjoyed a respectable position, was definitely subordinate to her husband."[24] The Hindu religious tradition up till today still bears this trace of the Aryan family life. As noted by Parrinder:

Certain fundamental characteristics of Hindu family law are traceable to the Aryan domestic religion. The head of the household was the priest of its religion, that is, the ancestor-cult; and inheritance of his property developed upon those competent to make offerings to him and his ancestors after his death, his married sons in the first instance.[25]

One needs only to look at Hinduism today to see the influence of the Aryan family life. The four stages of life in Hindu religious tradition is a development of the Aryan patriarchal family life.

Rebirth or Metempsychosis: One of the central doctrines of Hinduism today is rebirth or metempsychosis, simply put reincarnation. According Bala N. Aiyer, a modern Hindu scholar:

> Every Hindu believes in reincarnation of the soul who is born in this world again and again, to purify itself. They believe in the indestructibility of the soul of the individual (Jivatma) in reincarnation and rebirth. They believe in the soul travelling in an endless cycle of birth and death going between our world and the world of celestial beings or Heaven (Devaloka). Their aim and purpose are to perform certain karma and live according to the Svadharma so that they attain liberation and Moska.[26]

However, what is the origin of this belief? It goes back to Aryan culture as it mingled with the culture and belief of the Ganges Valley. According to Basham:

> As the Aryan culture pressed further down the Ganges it absorbed new ideas about after-life . . . In one of the late hymns[28]it is suggested in cryptic language that they [the dead] might pass to waters or remains in plants. This seems to be a reference to metempsychosis in the crude form believed by many primitive people, according the souls of the dead pass on to animal, plant or natural object, before being reborn in a human body . . . In the *Brahadarayaka* Upanishad the first form of the doctrine of transmigration is given.[29]

The refined doctrine of rebirth and reincarnation in Hinduism today is influenced by this ancient crude form of it and is derived from the Aryan culture.

Conclusion

The Aryan culture that came to India did not remain the same when it mingled with domestic culture and religion of the Indus and Ganges Valleys. It was also affected. Again, the religion it gave birth to, Brahmanism, which later became the basis of Hinduism also impacted on the culture. In order words, as culture impacts on religion so do religion impact and influence culture. It is a two-way traffic.

Although what is today called Hinduism was greatly influenced by the per-Aryan and Aryan cultures, what remains of Hinduism today still shows a remarkable difference from these ancient cultures. Parrinder makes this point clearer when he said that:

> If we compare the Hinduism of the past two thousand years with the religion of the Indo-Aryans, as it can be known from the Vedas, the contrasts are dramatic. Where the Hindus worships an iconic representative of the deity whom he or she chooses to regard as supreme, the Vedic Aryan had no icons and no personal relationship to a single supreme deity. Where the Hindus worship in a temple, Vedic religion had no temple, but centered about the sacred fire, in domestic hearth or on the brick out-of-doors altar. The Aryan pantheon was, with few exceptions, entirely male and predominantly celestial; the Hindu pantheon adds mother-goddesses, earth-goddesses, theomorphic divinities such as cobras, and tree-spirits.[29]

There are still many other differences, but whatever the case may be, present day Hinduism owes a lot of its traditions and practices to the pre-Aryan and Aryan cultures. This article goes to show how much impact culture can have on religion on the one hand, and how religion on the other hand becomes a vehicle for the transmission of culture to future generations. There is, therefore, a give and take relationship between culture and religion in general. This is not only seen in Hinduism but also including Judaism, Buddhism, Christianity, Islam, Confucianism, Taoism, Zoroastrianism, and indeed all the religions of the world.

NOTES.

1. *Encyclopedia Britannica of World Religions,* 1999.
2. Wilfred Cantwell Smith, *The Meaning and End of Religion.* (Minneapolis: Fortune Press, 1991), 53.
3. William Reese, *Dictionary of Philosophy and Religion.* (New York: Humanity Books, 1999), 151.
4. H. Richard Niebuhr, *Christ and Culture.* (New York: Harper and Row, 1951), 33.
5. Edward B. Tylor, *Primitive Culture.* (New York: J.P. Putnam & sons, 1920), 1.
6. Niebuhr, *Christ and Culture*, 33.
7. Ibid.
8. Duane E. Campbell, *Choosing Democracy: A practical guide to Multicultural Education, 3rd Ed.* (New Jersey: Prentice Hall, 2004), 43.
9. Clifford Geertz, *The Interpretation of Culture.* (New York: Basic Books, 1975), 89
10. Aylward Shorter, *Towards a Theology of Inculturation.* (New York: Orbis Books, 1997), 5.
11. Lewis M. Hopfe and Mark R. *Woodward, Religions of the World, 8th.* (New Jersey: Prentice Hall, 2001), 6.
12. Shorter, *Towards a Theology of Inculturation*, 80.
13. Geertz, *The Interpretation of Cultures*, 89-90, 113.
14. Geoffrey Parrinder, *World Religions: From Ancient History to the Present.* (New York: Facts On File, Inc., 1985), 213.
15. Thomas J. Hopkins, *The Hindu Religious Tradition.* (Belmont: Wadsworth Publishing Company, 1971), 8
16. Ibid, 11.

17. Ainslie T. Embree, *The Hindu Tradition: Readings in Oriental Thought*. (New York: Vintage Books, 1972), 4.

18. Hopfe & Woodward, *Religions of the World, 8th ed.*, 74.

19. Hopkins, *The Hindu Religious Tradition*, 9.

20. A L. Basham, *The Wonder that was India*. (New York: Grove Press, Inc., 1959), 298.

21. Hopfe & Woodward, *Religions of the World, 8th ed*, 72.

22. Basham, *The Wonder that was India*, 137.

23. Hopfe & Woodward, *Religions of the World, 8th ed*, 76.

24. Basham, The Wonder that was India, 239.

25. Ibid, 35.

26. Parrinder, *World Religions: From Ancient History to the Present*, 201

27. Bala N. Aiyer, *Principles and Practice of Hindu Religion* (Mumbai: Bhavan's Book University, 1999), 34.

28. The Hymn referred to here in this passage is the *Rig Veda X, 16.*

29. Basham, *The Wonder that was India*, 242.

30. Parrinder, *World Religions: From Ancient History to the Present*, 212.

1.3 THE CONCEPT AND PRACTICE OF SACRIFICE IN HINDU RELIGIOUS TRADITION.

Introduction.

Can we possibly think of a religion without the concept of sacrifice: sacrifice expressed in worship, rituals, offerings, and or devotions? The answer is "No." We can confidently assume that sacrifice is one of the most basic elements of religion. As observed by John Haught, sacrifice is one of the essential components of early religion[1], not just early religion but religions of today. Every religion has some act of sacrifice, which could be expressed outwardly or practiced inwardly. The concept of sacrifice implies giving up something, in most cases, for higher values. It could be directed to the divine beings or persons. Etymologically,

> The term *sacrifice,* from the Latin *sacrificium* (*sacre,* "holy"; *facere,* "to make"), carries the connotation of a religious act in the highest, or fullest sense; it can be understood as the act of sanctifying or consecrating an object. *Offering* is used as a synonym and means to present a gift. (The word *offering* is from the Latin *offerre,* "to offer, present"; the verb yields the noun *oblation.*)[2]

The intentions for which people offer sacrifices vary according to religions and individuals. As a general principle, "Theologians usually distinguish four intentions of sacrifice: praise (acknowledgement, homage), thanksgiving, supplication, and expiation; but several or even all four of these intentions may be combined in a single sacrifice."[3]

The focus of this essay is to explore the meaning of sacrifice and how it was practiced or performed, and probably still being practice, in the Hindu religious tradition. Sacrifice in Hindu religious tradition is a very broad area of scholarship, and so our focus in this exploration will center more on the Vedic tradition, although reference will be to other Post-Vedic traditions.

The Concept and Practice of Sacrifice in the Hindu Religious Tradition.

A synopsis of the concept and practice of sacrifice in the Hindu religious tradition is mainly contained in the one of most ancient sacred texts of Hinduism – the Veda. The part of the Vedic literature that deals with sacrificial rituals is the *Samhitās*, a collection of hymns that is divided into four parts namely: "the *Rig Veda, Yajur, Veda, Sāma Veda,* and *Artharva Veda.*"[4]

The Hindu word for sacrifice is *yajna*, a Sanskrit word from the verb root *yaj* "to worship". *Yajna,* understood as sacrifice and surrender through acts of worship, is a ritual form of worship especially prevalent in Vedic times, in which oblations – ghee, grains, spices and exotic woods – are offered into a fire according to scriptural injections while special mantras are chanted. In Hinduism, life is its totality is a sacrifice called *jivayajna*, a giving of oneself.[5] Central to the Hindu (Vedic) religious tradition was sacrifice, which could be private (household) or public. Reporting on the private or household sacrifice, Sri Swami Sivananda said:

> There are five great daily sacrifices that are performed by every householder. They are: (i) *Brahma Yajna*, called also Veda Yajna, sacrifice to Brahman or the Vedas or the Sages; (ii) *Deva Yajna*, sacrifice to the celestials; (iii) *Pitri Yajna*, sacrifice to the manes or offering libation to the forefathers; (iv) *Bhuta Yajna*, sacrifice to all creatures, i.e., food distribution to cows, dogs, birds, etc; and (v) *Manushya Yajna*, sacrifice to men, i.e., feeding the poor and the hungry, clothing the naked, giving shelter to the homeless, comforting the distress, etc.[6]

The most elaborate and ritualistic form of sacrifice is the public sacrifice, which generally revolves around Agni, the god of fire, who enjoys a dual role in Vedic traditions as both god and priest. According to Hopfe:

> Agni, the god of fire, is mentioned in over 200 hymns (in the Vedic literature). He is basically regarded as the

god of the priests and the priest of the gods. He leads the gods in proper sacrifice, and as the god of fire, he brings the burnt sacrifices to the other gods.[7]

The first hymn of the Rig Veda profusely extolled Agni as both priest and god. The hymn goes thus:

1. I laud Agni, the chosen Priest, God, minister of sacrifice, the hotar, lavishest of wealth. 2. Worthy is Agni to be praised by living as by ancient seers. He shall bring hitherward the Gods. 3. Through Agni man obtaineth wealth, yea, plenty waxing day by day, Most rich in heroes, glorious. 4. Agni, the perfect sacrifice which thou encompassest about Verily goeth to the Gods. 5. May Agni, sapient-minded Priest, truthful, most gloriously great, The God, come hither with the Gods. 6. Whatever blessing, Agni, thou wilt grant unto thy worshipper, That, Aṅgiras, is indeed thy truth. 7. To thee, dispeller of the night, O Agni, day by day with prayer bringing thee reverence, we come. 8. Ruler of sacrifices, guard of Law eternal, radiant One, Increasing in thine own abode. 9 Be to us easy of approach, even as a father to his son: Agni, be with us for our weal.[8]

In the Hindu sacrifice, fire (sacred fire) occupies a primary place of importance. This element of Hindu sacrificial life is influenced by the Aryan religious and Vedic life, which is increasingly dominated by fire sacrifice; the creative source of all the powers of nature and the gods.[9]

As there are complexities and multiplicities of gods in the Hindu religious tradition, so there are forms and methods of sacrifice. In this essay, we shall only mentioned few of them, namely the horse sacrifice, the human sacrifice of Shunahshepa, and animal sacrifice. According to Wendy Doniger:

> The horse sacrifice was the most elaborate of all Vedic sacrifices, performed by a great king to establish his supremacy and to ensure the prosperity and fertility of his kingdom. Though it was seldom performed

even in ancient times, it remained the most important paradigm both for sacrifice and for kingship throughout Hindu literature . . . Four main priests officiate at the sacrifice . . . The human sacrifice of Shunahshpa involves substituting the human person with a surrogate (an animal) . . . Animal sacrifices play a part in many sorts of rituals. Animal sacrifice takes place in the course of the initiation of a Vaishnava pupil by his guru.[10]

The Essence of Sacrifice in the Hindu Religious Tradition.

Sacrifices are offered for many varied reasons in Vedic (Hindu) religious traditions. The main reason among other things is the creation and maintenance of the cosmic order. According to Embree, "The concepts and practices of the sacrificial ritual, which was at the heart of Vedic religion, were also linked to the fundamental understanding of the existence of a cosmic law."[11] Hence, "The belief grew up that the sacrifice was necessary for the maintenance of the cosmic order, and that without regular sacrifice all cosmic process would cease, and chaos would come again."[12]

Sacrifices in Hindu religious tradition are offered for the purpose of pleasing or placating the gods in order to receive various kinds of favor. They are offered also for atonement for wrong doings, and as a thank-offering for favors already received. The *Yajur Veda* gives us a clue as essence of sacrifice and what is offered for what purpose:

He who desires prosperity should offer a white (beast) to Vayu;. He who desires offspring should offer to Vayu of the team; He who has long been ill should offer to Vayu of the team; He who desires offspring and cattle should offer to Prajapati a hornless goat. He who desires cattle should offer one of a triplet to Soma and Pusan; the she-goat has two teats, two are born separately, the third for strength and growth.[13]

Sacrifices are also offered for protection. Again, the *Yajur Veda* gives us a clue:

Thou, O Soma, art the giver of wide protection from hostility, brought about by ourselves or by others; hail! May the active one gladly partake of the ghee. May Agni here make room for us; May he go before us cleaving the foe; joyously may he conquer our foes.[14]

Conclusion.

A careful analysis of sacrifice in the Vedic (Hindu) religious tradition reveals that efficacy of the sacrifice does not necessarily depend on the disposition gods, nor does it depend on the sacrificial objects. It depends essentially on the right use of the rituals. In this case, it depends on the sacrificer, that is, the Brahman or priest. The Brahman as "the custodian of the sacrifice"[15] occupies an indispensible place in the sacrificial rituals that even the gods depend on him. As observed by Embree:

If the sacrifice was properly performed the gods could not withhold the boon requested. The sacrifice was understood to be able to provide the desired result, and the will of the gods became almost irrelevant . . . The priest therefore became a key figure in the whole drama of the cosmic order . . . From this the conclusion was drawn that what was important was not the gods to whom the sacrifice was made, nor the materials of the materials of the sacrifice, but the sacrificer, who knew the secret formulae that held the cosmos together.[16]

From this exposition it is clear that the Vedic concept of sacrifice differs in some ways from the Judeo-Christian concept of sacrifice, which is always "God-oriented, based in the fact and value of God's relationship with his people, and his covenant."[17] Here, God has the absolute disposition to grant or not to what is asked for, unlike the Vedic sacrifice where the will of the gods are tied the ritual aptitude of the priest.

NOTES

1. John F. Haught, *What is Religion: An Introduction.* (New York: Paulist Press, 1990), 24.

2. Joseph Henninger, "Sacrifice" in *Encyclopedia of Religion.* Ed. Lindsay Jones. Vol. 12. 2nd ed. (Detroit: Macmillan Reference USA, 2005), 7997.

3. Ibid, 8001

4. Ainslie T. Embree, *The Hindu Tradition: Readings in Oriental Thought.* (New York: Vintage Books, 1972), 5.

5. Sacrifice: Hindu – Hinduism Dictionary on Sacrifice. http://www.experiencefestival.com/a/sacrifice/id/61903 (accessed September 4, 2008)

6. Sri Swami Sivananda, Pancha MahaYajnas: *The Hindu Ritual Pancha MahaYajnas.* http://www.experiencefestival.com/a/Pancha_Mahayajnas/id/23095 (accessed September 4, 2008)

7. Lewis M. Hopfe & Mark R. *Woodward, Religions of the World, 8th ed.* (New Jersey: Prentice Hall, 2001), 79.

8. Rig Veda, I, 1, 1-9.

9. Thomas J. Hopkins, *The Hindu Religious Tradition.* (Belmont, CA: Wadsworth Publishing Company, 1971), 17.

10. Wendy Doniger O'Flaherty, Ed. *Textual Sources for the Study of Hinduism.* (Chicago: The University of Chicago Press, 1988), 7,19,84.

11. Embree, *The Hindu Tradition: Readings in Oriental Thought,* 11.

12. A. L. Basham, *The Wonder that was India.* (New York: Grove Press, 1959), 239.

13. Yajur Veda ii. 1.1

14. Yajur Veda, i. 3.4

15. Geoffrey Parrinder, *World Religions: From Ancient History to the Present.* (New York: Fact on File, 1985), 201

16. Embree, *The Hindu Tradition: Readings in Oriental Thought,* 27-28, 11.

17. Francis X. Clooney, "Sacrifice and its Spiritualization in the Christian and Hindu Traditions: A Study in Comparative Theology", in *The Harvard Theological Review, vol. 78, No.3/4* (Cambridge University Press, Jul. –Oct.,1985), pp. 361-380

1.4 EXPLAINING THE HINDU CONCEPTS OF KARMA, SAMSARA, DUHKHA (PALI: DUKKHA), AND MOKSA AND HOW THESE CONCEPTS ARE RELATED TO ONE ANOTHER

Introduction

Hinduism is perhaps the most complex of all the world's major religions, comprising a multiplicity of cults and sects, with many gods. Unlike other religions, it has no particular founder and no defining creed. Nevertheless, there are doctrines that most Hindu devotees share in common irrespective of sect and cult. Among these are the concepts of *Karma, Samsara, Duhkha, and Moksa.* These doctrines became evident in the *Upanishads,* which later influenced Hindu traditions.

Karma

The Sanskrit word *Karma* literally refers to an act and by extension implies the effects or fruits of that action. It designates action and reaction on all levels comprising "our past thoughts, words and deeds."[1] Karma goes beyond the simple notion of cause and effect. In Hindu thought, it is regarded as a "powerful and elusive energy within the human person, *jiva.*"[2] Although implied in the Vedas, "the concept of *Karma* was well established in the early Upanishads,"[3] and with the Upanishads, it gained ground in Indian tradition very rapidly in the 7th and 6th centuries B.C.[4]

Hindu thinkers distinguish three kinds of *karma* namely:

> *Sañcita, prārabdha,* and *āgāmi. Sañcita* is all the accumulated karma of the past. Part of it is seen in the character of the individual, his tendencies and aptitude, inclinations and desires etc. *Prārabdha* is that portion of the past karma which is responsible for the present body. *Āgāmi* is the coming karma, which includes also the karma that is being gathered at present.[5]

In Hinduism, the concept of *karma* (action) is linked up with the concept *dharma* (duty) and has a part to play in the maintenance of the cosmic order. As expressed by Rinehart,

> Karma binds together an individual's *dharma* in the past, present, and future. Thus *karma* not only provides the acceptance of one's way of life in this present life but also provides an incentive to act according to dharma and reap its result in the future . . . When we act, then, we participate in a cosmic process of either purifying or polluting ourselves or the world around us.[6]

Karma explains why people are born differently and behave differently in Hindu tradition and society.

Samsara.

The term *Samsara* is a Sanskrit word that denotes the cycle of existence, with its implication of repeated birth and death. An Indologist, Louis Renou, defined samsara as the "indefinite transmigration of living beings until release is achieved."[7] Hinduism believes that the life force of an individual (atman, soul) does not die with the death of the body, but instead moves on to another time and body where it continues to live.

Although the concept of the soul (atman) as the undying life principle was already seen in the Vedas, samara as the "endless rebirth of the soul appeared explicitly in the Upanishads. The two fullest accounts are in the *Brihadaranyaka* (6.2.9-16) and *Chandogya* (5.4.1-5.10.8) *Upanishads.*"[8]

In Hindu thought, the concept of samsara, understood as reincarnation in the western world, does not exist on its own. Rather, it is understood and explained in relation to the concept of karma. As noted by Sharma:

> If one accepts the view, as most Hindus do, that we continually undergo reincarnation, then the question arises: what determines where, how we will be incarnated,

and what will befall us in that incarnation? The answer to this question in a word is: Karma![9]

In Indian thought, this cycle of birth and rebirth is seen as a punishment. In Western language, *Samsara* is also expressed as metempsychosis (transmigration of the soul).

Duhkha.

The Sanskrit word *duhkha,* Pali: *dukkha* 'literarily means 'pain', 'suffering', 'despair', 'sorrow', or 'misery.' This concept implies the fact of human existence: that life or existence is characterized by suffering"[10]

This concept in Hinduism states that while in *samsara,* one is a state of constant suffering. In other words, the continuous process of birth, death and rebirth causes suffering. Although *dukkha* is literarily interpreted as suffering, its religious meaning goes beyond suffering in the ordinary sense of every day physical, mental pain, and emotional deprivations that cause pain; it includes suffering through change, that is, unsatisfactoriness, imperfections, and impermanence of all things, conditioned existence, and the non realization of liberation.[11]

Moksa.

The Sanskrit term *moksa* is variously translated as immortality, salvation, liberation, release, self-realization and God-realization.[12] In the view of Sharma:

> The word moksa means freedom or emancipation. This naturally raises the question: Freedom from what? The answer then usually given is: Freedom from *samsara* (the cycle of birth and rebirth). *Moksa* is the quintessential concept of Hinduism. It means that the *jiva* has crossed over the line from the mundane to the divine by pursuing one of the *yogas* successfully. The form of *moksa* may be a matter of difference of opinion (E.g., the Advaita Vedanta philosophers maintain that *moksa*

is a state of bliss, contrary to those who see it as a state of absence of pain and suffering, and union of the atman with Brahman) but all agree on its effect: cessation of rebirth, of samsara.[13]

Again, Hindu thinkers generally identify four various types of moksa: *sāyujya* (union or absorption), *sālokya* (place in the Lord's world), *sāmīpya* (proximity), and *sārūpya* (attaining same form as god).[14] The different types of *moksa* identified by Hindu thinkers, not withstanding, is a "wide range of agreement that *moksa* is not a state of affairs that arises only after death, but that one can in fact attain moksa while living (*jivanmukti*)"[15]

The Relationship between the Four Concepts

These four concepts together form the basis of Hindu religious belief. They are so interrelated that none exists without the other. One is either the cause or the consequence of the other. The concept of *karma* gives rise to the concept of *samsara*. Samsara causes dukkha, and *moksa* brings cessation of *duhkha* by liberating one from the pains of *samsara*. It goes like this: every individual soul undergoes the process of countless births and rebirths (*samsara*) to perform proper *karma* to purify itself. This process of birth and rebirth ties the individual to the state of *dukkha*, a state that can only be freed from the realization of *moksa* (release). To express this in the words of Aiyer,

> The Hindus believe that every soul has to go through some suffering (*dukkha)* for their wrong deeds as their *Karma*. So the soul gets reborn again and again (samsara) to purify itself by good *karma* and ultimately reaches *moksa* which is union with the Almighty God (Brahman).[16]

These concepts were impressively brought out as related to each other for the first time in Hindu tradition in the *Upanishads*. In this Vedic literature, the soul "repeatedly dies and is reborn, causing it repeated or endless suffering and misery; the cause of this is the effect of ones deeds in this or past life, and there is an escape from the weary round of death and rebirth.(*moksa, nirvana*)."[17]

Conclusion.

It is worth mentioning that these four concepts are not limited to Hinduism alone. Originating from the Hindu tradition, these were imbibed by other religions that originated in India in the 6th century BCE. Ancient as they are, these four concepts are still being believed today in these religions as facts of life and the goal of human life. To end with the words of Hopfe, "Indeed, the goal of most Indian religions is to break the cycle of *karma* and *samsara* and be free from the burden of life (*dukkha*). This breaking free from the burden of life is called *moksa*."[18]

NOTES
1. Susunaga Weeraperuma, *Nirvana: The Highest Happiness.* (New Delhi: Vedams Books, 2003), 31.
2. Ibid, 32.
3. Ainslie Embree, *The Hindu Tradition: Readings in Oriental Thought.* (New York: Vintage Books, 1972), 62
4. A. L. Bashan, *The Wonder that was India.* (New York: Grove Press, Inc., 1959), 242
5. T. M. P. Mahadevan, *Outlines of Hinduism.* (Bombay: Chetna Ltd, 1971), 60.
6. Robin Rinehart, *Contemporary Hinduism: Ritual, Culture, and Practice.* (Oxford: ABC-CLIO, Inc, 2004), 103,165.
7. Louis Renou, *Hinduism.* (New York: George Braziller, 1962), 43.
8. Steve Collins, *Selfless Person.* (Cambridge: Cambridge University Press, 1982), 51.
9. Arvind Sharma, *Classical Hindu Thought: An Introduction.* (New Delhi: Oxford University Press, 2000), 98.

10. Thomas J. Hopkins, *The Hindu Religious Tradition*. (Belmont: Wadsworth Pub. Co., 1971), 56.

11. Collins, *Selfless Person*, 191-192

12. Rinehart, *Contemporary Hinduism: Ritual, Culture, and Practice*, 160

13. Sharma, *Classical Hindu Thought: An Introduction*, 113.

14. Ibid, 117.

15. Rinehart, *Contemporary Hinduism: Ritual, Culture, and Practice*, 161

16. Bala N. Aiyer, *Principles and Practice of Hindu Religion*. (Mumbai: Bhavan's Book University, 1999), 23.

17. Geoffrey Parrinder, *World Religions: From Ancient History to the Present*. (New York: Facts On File, Inc., 1985), 209.

18. Hopfe &. Woodward, *Religions of the World*, 8th. 83.

1.5 THE EXCELLENCE OF BHAKTI YOGA OVER KARMA YOGA AND JNANA YOGA IN THE BHAGAVAD-GITA. (A COMPARATIVE ANALYSIS OF THE YOGIC PRACTICE IN HINDUISM).

Introduction.

The yogic practice, as a way of attaining liberation and salvation in Hinduism was developed in the later Vedic literature, especially the late Upanishads. The word yoga is derived from the "root word *yuj*, which means to "yoke" or "harness," and carries the general connotation of "joining" or "uniting oneself with."[1] In the Upanishads, "Yoga was understood as a mental disciple of the senses, mind and intellect; it is the discipline that the higher powers of the body enforce upon the lower ones, aimed at bringing the whole body to a state of quiescence so that the self may be truly free."[2] Particular attention was given to the Karma Yoga (way of action) and Jnana Yoga (way of Knowledge) in earlier traditions. At this point in the Hindu religious life, the way of devotion (Bhakti Yoga) as a separate way of attainment of salvation was not well developed, if known at all. This concept and way of life was developed and extolled in the *Bhagavad-Gita*.

In this essay, our concern is to examine the religious concept and understanding of Karma and Jnana yoga, and the eventual excellence given to Bhakti, (devotion) over the two previous Hindu religious practices as contained in the *Bhagavad-Gita*. To do this, we shall begin with a brief overview of the *Bhagavad-Gita* as a Hindu sacred text.

The *Bhagavad-Gita*: An Overview.

The *Bhagavad-Gita*, literally translated as the *Song of God*, is part of the Hindu Epic, the *Mahabharata*, whose "central theme is the great war between the sons of the two royal brothers,"[3] namely, "the Pandavas and the Kauravas."[4] The Pandavas and the Kauravas are also referred to as "the Dhrtarastra and Pandu, who were brothers born in the Kuru dynasty, descending from King

Bharata."[5]According to tradition, the *Gita* was primarily spoken by the Lord to His disciple, the sun-god Vivasvan, at least 120,400,000 years ago. It was respoken by the Lord Krishna again to Arjuna about 5000 years ago.[6]

The story of the Gita is the climax of the war situation between the Pandavas and the Kauravas.[7] The main characters are Arjuna, a Pandava warrior, and Krishna, his charioteer. Arjuna, divided between fighting and killing his kinsmen and fulfilling his class obligation (dharma) as a warrior, was enlightened by Krishna, who revealed himself as the Supreme Lord of the Universe. In the process of the dialogue between Krishna and Arjuna, Krishna not rejecting the Upanishads' yogic practices of jnana (knowledge) and karma (action), led Arjuna to a higher and more excellent form of yoga, namely bhakti (love or devotion) According to Hopkins:

> Krishna begins his instruction by teaching Arjuna the 'discipline of knowledge' (jnana-yoga) and 'the discipline of action' (karma-yoga) to correct Arjuna's initial confusion . . . The way of bhakti is developed gradually in the Gita as Arjuna becomes aware of Krishna's divine status . . . Krishna is revealed [to Arjuna] as the Supreme Lord, identified with the Vedic Brahman and Purusa and with the universal form of Vishnu. He is the culmination of all the religious forms of the Vedas, but these forms are subsumed under a new conception of God and a new way of salvation . . . Krishna is God among men, born to restore righteousness in the world and make salvation more accessible. The impersonal Brahman of the Upanishads is not rejected, nor [sic] earlier ways of salvation, but alongside them, the Gita offers what is declared as a better way, easier and more open to all who will join in devotion [bhakti] to the Lord.[8]

The Hindu Yoga (Karma, Jnana, and Bhakti) In the *Gita*.
The Vedic literature developed different ways of living and practicing religion. One of these ways, as already noted, is the practice of yoga, which includes the karma, jnana, and bhakti. In the Vedas and the Upanishads, bhakti was subordinate to the other ways, but in the *Gita*, it was extolled as the most excellent way of practicing religion. To get a clear picture of this, we shall begin this section by briefly explaining what these ways mean, especially in the understanding of the *Gita*.

Karma Yoga (the path of action): The word karma literarily means "deed", "work", or "action", and is used in Hindu tradition to mean both any action which produces tendencies or impressions (*sanskaras)* in the actor, which then function as determinants to his future action, and specific ritual actions which are performed in the context of Vedic ceremonial religion."[9] In the *Gita*, Karma yoga entails that everyone must engage in some sort of activity in this material world. However, actions can only be a means of liberation if the actor does not attach himself to the fruits of his action, that is to say, "By acting for the pleasure of the Supreme, without selfish motives, one can be liberated from the law of karma (action and reaction) and attain transcendental knowledge of the self and the Supreme."[10]

> **Jnana Yoga (the path of knowledge):** The word Jnana literarily means: knowledge, intuition, spiritual understanding and is often used in conjunction with yoga to denote the spiritual path by means of which men of strong and intellectual or philosophical (sattvic) disposition seek self-realization. Jnana yoga is the discipline associated most closely with Advaita Vedanta, the non-dualistic system expounded primarily by Shankara . . . The Gita speaks highly of this path but suggests that in its pure form it is only meaningful for only a very few persons, and that by itself it cannot lead to the special sort of world-affirmation with which the Gita is concerned.11

Jnana yoga as a religious practice is the purest form and most difficult way of Hindu spiritual life, and cannot be practiced by people attached to their daily duties.

Bhakti Yoga (the path of devotion): Literarily, Bhakti means, love or devotion. It is the loving adoration for a personal divinity, as a means of obtaining unity with the Divine Being to whom the devotion is directed. In the *Gita*, bhakti yoga is the means by which people are able to plumb the depths of religious experience.[12] Bhakti yoga is pure devotional service to the Lord Krishna. It is regarded as highest and most expedient means for attaining pure love for Krishna, which is the highest end of spiritual existence.

The Excellence of Bhakti over Jnana and Karma Yoga.

The Lord Krishna in the Gita led Arjuna to the knowledge that of the entire paths to salvation available to the Hindus, the most excellent is pure and total devotion to him, Krishna, as the Supreme Lord of the Universe. The two other ways, (karma and Jnana) are not condemned by Krishna in the Gita, but there are more or less deficient as a way of attaining liberation and union with God. In the Gita, 6:46-47, Krishna said:

> The yogin, [who is devoted to me] is greater that the ascetic, he is thought to be greater that even the wise; the yogin is greater than men of ritual action; therefore be a yogin, O Arjuna. And of all yogins, the one who, full of faith worships me with his inner self abiding in me, he is the thought by me to be the most disciplined.[13]

Again, Bhakti yoga is extolled and valued above other ways because it is open to all. It does not discriminate against women or caste system, unlike the other ways that exclude women and those of lower caste. Moreover, Bhakti yoga does not require any observance of ritual purity and intense mediation or practice. Expressing this in the words of Hopkins, "It [Bhakti] is thus ideally suited to the needs of lower classes and householders for whom the traditional ideal of a renounced life as an ascetic was at best a far-off hope."[14] In Chapter 9:29-32, Krishna declared:

> I am equal to all beings; there is none hateful to me nor dear to me. But those who worship me with devotion, they are in me and I am in them. Even if a man of evil conduct worships me with undivided devotion, he too must be considered righteous, for he has resolved rightly. Quickly he become a righteous self and obtains eternal peace; O son of Kunti, know thou that my devotee never perishes. They who take refuge in me, O Partha, even though they be born of sinful wombs, women, Vaishyas, and even Shudras, they also reach the highest goal.[15]

Commenting on the excellence of Bhakti yoga over other ways, Hopkins opined that the true man of knowledge, as defined by Krishna, is not the traditional possessor of Vedic wisdom, but the one characterized by single-minded devotion to him. Also the impersonal Brahman of the Upanishad is not rejected, nor is earlier ways of salvation, but along side them, the *Gita* offers what is declared as a better way, easier and more open to all who will join in devotion to the Lord.[16] Thus, Bhakti directed to Krishna becomes the highest form of yoga far above karma and jnana yoga, and this enjoyed a great popularity among the Hindus and was followed by many.[17]

Conclusion.

The primacy given to Bhakti yoga, understood as an act of faith expressed in devotion to the Lord Krishna, over karma (action or work) and jnana (knowledge) recalls to me the theology of the reformation expounded by Martin Luther, John Calvin, Zwingli and other protestant reformers of the 16th century. Contrary to the Catholic teaching that salvation is achieved through one's good deeds combined with faith in God, the reformers taught was is called *sola fides* – only by faith in Jesus Christ alone can one attain salvation. The *Gita* to me seems a protest to the traditional way of life and salvation in Vedic tradition. Again, in the *Gita*, the sacramental-sacrificial elements of the Vedic tradition are replaced with the non-sacramental devotion to Krishna. Again, this recalls the shift in the pre-reformation Christian Liturgical worship that revolves around the sacrifice of the Mass to the post-reformation Protestant service that excludes the sacrifice of the Mass and centers only on the bible and devotional services.

NOTES

1. Eliot Deutsch, *Trans. The Bhagavad-Gita.* (New York: University Press of America, 1968), 6.
2. Thomas J. Hopkins, *The Hindu Religious Tradition.* (Belmont: Wadsworth Publishing Company, 1971), 65.
3. Ainslie T. Embree, *The Hindu Tradition: Readings in Oriental Thought.* (New York: Vintage Books, 1972), 138.
4. Wendy Doniger O'Flaherty, *Ed. Textual Sources for the Study of Hinduism.* (Chicago: The University of Chicago Press, 1988), 46.
5. A. C. Bhaktivedanta Swami Prabhupada, *Bhagavad-Gita As It Is.* (Los Angeles: The Bhaktivedanta Book Trust, 1986), xiii.
6. Ibid, 217.
7. James Fieser and John Powers, *Scriptures of the World Religions. 2nd Ed.* (New York: McGraw Hill, 2004), 38.
8. Hopkins, *The Hindu Religious Tradition* ,92,94
9. Deutsch, *The Bhagavad-Gita,* 12-13.
10. Prabhupada, *Bhagavad-Gita As It Is,* viii.
11. Deutsch, *The Bhagavad-Gita,* 14-15.
12. Ibid, 15.
13. Deutsch, *The Bhagavad-Gita,* 71.
14. Hopkins, *The Hindu Religious Tradition,* 94.
15. Deutsch, *The Bhagavad-Gita,* 86.
16. Hopkins, *The Hindu Religious Tradition,* 93-94.
17. K. M. Sen, *Hinduism* (Baltimore: Penguin Books, 1961), 9

CHAPTER TWO

ESSAYS ON BUDDHISM

2.1 BUDDHISM: BRIEF HISTORICAL FACTS.

Buddhism originated in India, with Siddhartha Gautama as its founder. Siddhartha Gautama later became known as the BUDDHA, meaning the "Enlightened One." The Buddha lived between c. 563-483 BC, making Buddhism a religion of more than 2,500 years old.

Buddhism does not have one official scripture. There are many Sacred texts known as the Sutras that are recognized as Scriptures by different Buddhist Traditions. Generally, Buddhism is divided into two major traditions: The Theravada tradition and the Mahayana tradition. Buddhism is an a-theistic religion; it does not worship nor does it revolve around the concept of a God. It is the fourth largest religion in the world today, with an estimated population of 353 Million adherents

2.2 THE BUDDHIST DOCTRINE OF "NO-SELF" (AN-ATMAN) SALVATION, AND ITS PROBLEM FOR CONTEMPORARY BUDDHISTS.

Introduction.

Besides the absence of a belief in a universal God, one doctrine which separates Buddhism from all other religions, creeds, and systems of philosophy is the doctrine of an-atman (no-self), which is the denial of the "Soul, Self, Ego, or to use Sanskrit expression *Atman*, as a permanent, everlasting, and absolute entity."[1] This doctrine of an-atman, the bedrock of Buddhism, presents utmost difficulty to many people including Buddhists. What is the essential content of this doctrine according the Buddha and Buddhist thinkers? What message did the Buddha hope to get across to his followers in the doctrine, and why is it problematic to later Buddhists? These questions will be addressed in this paper.

The Essential Content of the Doctrine of *An-Atman*.

The Buddhist term *An-atman* (Sanskrit) or *Anatta* (Pali) is literally used to refer to the nature of phenomena as being devoid of the Soul or Self. Specifically, an-atman denotes the temporal and unreal nature of all composite, consubstantial, phenomenal, and temporal things, from the macrocosmic, to microcosmic, be it matter as pertains the physical body, the cosmos at large, including any and all mental machinations which are of the nature of arising and passing.[2] As expressed by Collins:

> An-atman is a description applied to all phenomena and objects of thought. In Buddhism, it applies to any and every item of the Buddhist conceptual universe (*dhamma*), whether parts of the karmic conditioning process or the unconditioned *nibbana*: impermanent are all conditioned things, unsatisfactory, not-self, and constructed; and certainly, *nibbana* also is a description meaning not-self.[3]

Essentially, the doctrine of *an-ātman* specifies the absence of a permanent and unchanging self or soul. It implies the Buddha's denial of the "the soul, the individual self, the ego, the I-ness, the My-ness or any permanent entity which governs within and receives rewards and retribution for one's action."[4] What is normally thought of as the "self" is in fact an agglomeration of "five attributes (*skandhas*) namely: form (*rupa*), sensation (*vedana*), perception (*sanna*), volition (*sankhara*), and consciousness (*vinnana*)."[5] These are constantly changing physical and mental constituents, which give rise to unhappiness if clung to as though this temporary assemblage formed some kind of immutable and enduring Soul. As taught by the Buddha:

> Though both body and mind appear because of cooperating cause, it does not follow that there is an ego-personality. As the body of flesh is an aggregate of elements, it is, therefore, impermanent. If a man believes that such an impermanent thing, (self or soul) so changeable and filled with suffering, is the ego-personality, it is a serious mistake.[6]

The Buddhist doctrine *an-atman* is use synonymously with "*anicca*" which denotes that impermanence is the inexorable, fundamental and pitiless law of all existence.

Practically, *an-atman* is inseparable from *anicca.*"[7]

The Intention of the Doctrine With Reference To the Buddha's Doctrine of Salvation.

The intention of the Buddha in this doctrine was not for his followers to doubt their existence. For, to believe that they do not exist would amount to an annihilation theory; and to believe firmly that they exist would equally amount to an eternalist theory. Rather, the *an-atman* doctrine is meant "to act, or thought to, as an agent of spiritual change"[8] in the Buddhist practitioner so that the "realization of *anatta*, which is the loss of pride or conceit, will constitute the attainment of Arhatship."[9]

Again, a deep understanding of the doctrine of an-atman is "an essential prerequisite for the attainment of Nirvana,"[10] because in this, the practitioner is detached from misplaced clinging to what is mistakenly regarded as his or her Self. A good example of how the doctrine of an-atman is essential for the attainment of Nirvana is given in the *Cularahulovada sutta*. In this sutta, as cited by Weeraperuma, the Buddha addressed the doctrine of an-atman to the Venerable Rahula at Savatthi. Rahula realized the truth that is inherent in this 'no-self' teaching. He became disenchanted with his sense organs and state of consciousness, which resulted in dispassion and calmness. Ceasing to cling to anything, he attained the peace of Nirvana.[11]

Expressing the Buddha's intention in another way, Guruge said:

> The doctrine of Anatta is aimed at dispelling this feeling or thought of *"I am"*, which is the cause of "becoming" and its consequences of suffering through birth, sickness, decay, death and so forth. The Buddha sought to drive home the futility of feeling of *"I am"*, by showing how that *"I"* could neither govern nor predetermine the way the aggregates arose and perished . . . With the doctrine of Anatta, the Buddha laid the foundation for his ethical mission. Its ultimate goal is deliverance, salvation or emancipation of humans from the cycle of birth and death.[12]

The Problem of This Doctrine for Contemporary Buddhists.

One of the reasons why the doctrine of *an-atman* became so problematic for later Buddhists comes from the Buddhists Canon itself. In some texts, *atman* is completely denied, and in some texts, it does not seem to be denied out rightly. Commenting on this problem, Collins observed that:

> A study of the canonical texts shows clearly that the denial of self, the refusal to allow any 'ultimate' validity

to personal terms that are taken to refer to anything real
and permanent, is insisted on only in certain specific
kind of conceptually sophisticated theoretical context.
The linguistic items translated lexically as 'self' and
'person' (in Pali *atta, purisa/puggala*, Sanskrit *atman,
purusa/pudgala* respectively) are used quite naturally and
freely in a number of contexts, without any suggestion
that their being so used might conflict with the doctrine
of *anatta*.[13]

Again later Buddhists encounter an intellectual quandary with
the teaching because the doctrine of *an-atman* and the doctrine of
rebirth (*samsara*) seem to be mutually exclusive. If there is no self,
no abiding essence of the person, what then is it that is reborn?

However, some Buddhist scholars do not see much problem
in the seemingly contradictory texts on the doctrine of at-man
in the Buddhist canon and sutta. The problem is explained using
another Buddhist doctrine: *Upaya* – Skillful Means. According to
Khantipalo:

> Unless this skillful Means is taken into account, one
> who investigates Buddhist Teachings through original
> scriptures might suppose that there were all sorts of
> contradictions. It should be clearly understood that it
> makes all the difference to the type of teaching given,
> whether it is addressed to a monk, or to a layman, to one
> devoted to the Lord's teaching or to an outsider.[14]

Conclusion.

The problem inherent in this teaching not withstanding,
consciousness of the egolessness and the impermanent of all things
will assist Buddhists to avoid attachment to the self and desire, thereby
avoiding suffering, death, and rebirth. It helps the Buddhists to see
things as they really are. This knowledge and understanding of things
in their true nature is essential for the attainment of enlightenment
and the subsequent realization of Nirvana or salvation.

It should be pointed out that the doctrine of *an-atman* does not say or imply simply that the Soul or self (atta, Atman) has no reality, but that certain things (5 aggregates), with which the unenlightened identifies himself, are not the Soul (anatta) and that is why one should grow disgusted with them, become detached from them and be liberated. It can be said that the doctrine of an-atman is "not a doctrine of 'no-soul', but what the 'soul is not' (form is an-atman, feelings are an-atman, etc.)"[15]

Notes.
1. Steven Collins, *Selfless PersoN*. (Cambridge: Cambridge University Press, 1982), 4.
2. Ananda K. Coomaraswamy, *Buddha and the Gospel of Buddhism*. (Delhi: Munshiram Manoharlal Publishers,1974), 88
3. Collins, *Selfless Person*, 96.
4. Ananda W. Guruge, *What in Brief is Buddhism*. (Hacienda Heights: Buddha's Light publishing, 2004), 34.
5. Susunaga Weeraperuma, *Nirvana: The Highest Happiness*. (New Delhi: Vedams Books, 2003), 56.
6. Bukkyo Dendo Kyokai, *The Teaching of the Buddha*. (Tokyo: Kosaido Printing Co., 2004), 46-47.
7. Coomaraswamy, *Buddha and the Gospel of Buddhism*, 84,88.
8. Collins, *Selfless Person*, 152
9. Ibid, 94.
10. Weeraperuma, *Nirvana: The Highest Happiness*, 171.
11. Ibid,
12. Guruge, What in Brief is Buddhism? 37-38.
13. Collins, *Selfless Person*, 71.
14. Khantipalo Bhikkhu, *Buddhism Explained*, (Bangkok: Social Science Ass. Press, 1968), 19-20.
15. Re-establishing the correct doctrinal definition of ANATTA/ANATMAN in Buddhism, Neo-Vedanta via negative. http://newsgroups.derkeiler.com/Archive/Talk/talk.religion.buddhism/2008-02/msg00174.html (accessed: February 8, 2009)

2.3 THE INFLUENCE OF CULTURE ON RELIGION (WITH PARTICULAR REFERENCE TO BUDDHISM IN CHINA).

Introduction.

In a community or society, what to do people first meet: culture or religion? To answer this question, let us look at a very beautiful picturesque intellectual scene created by John F. Haught, who challenged us to:

> Picture the following scenes. Cave dwellers in Western Europe 35,500 years ago are burying one of the children of their tribe, taking pains to arrange the body in a deliberate pattern, and adoring it with special ornaments and pigmentation. An aged ascetic in India sits quietly in contemplation at the edge of a forest . . . Such gestures usually goes by the name "religion."[1]

Are these expressing simply a religion or primarily a cultural system handed down from generations? The answer is that they are first expressing a culture, a way of the people's life. To support this, Wilfred Cantwell Smith said:

> First let us note the noncivilizational people of the world: those who in their small communities and with their nonliterary traditions have provided the source material for the many informative studies of what used to be called primitive religion . . . Yet none, apparently, has traditionally had a name for that system. Nor have these groups a term for religion in general. *The persons concerned will say,* 'It is our custom [culture] to . . . ,'[2]

From the above quotations, it can be said that religion generally is influenced by culture. The cultural system of a particular society shapes the religion that emerges or takes root within that society; the religion on the other hand equally shapes the culture. This is true also of Buddhism particularly as it spread and took root in China. The question here is: how is this true of Buddhism?

To address this question, we shall begin by defining culture and religion.

Culture: A Definition.

The term culture has been variously defined and understood by many scholars, each from the viewpoint of his or her own field of scholarship. Etymologically, the term culture is derived:

> From the Latin *colere* meaning 'to till or cultivate'. The term is sometimes used to include all of the creative expressions of man in all fields of human endeavor. At other times it is confined to creative expression in the areas of the liberal arts. In the second of these senses the term is sometimes extended to personal cultivation.[3]

It is generally believed that culture is the way a particular people believe, behave, act and live. In other words, it is a way of life. It is humans that define culture, without humans there is no culture. Expressed in another way, culture is the totality of patterns according to which human beings think, act and feel. It is the channel through which people view the whole of their experience. Accordingly, Niebuhr said,

> Culture is the work of men's minds and hands. It is that portion of man's heritage in any place and time that has been given us designedly and laboriously by other men, not what has come to us via the mediation of nonhuman beings.[4]

One of the most celebrated definitions of culture is that given by the renowned sociologist, Edward Tylor. He defined culture as "that complex whole which includes knowledge, belief, art, morals, laws customs and any other capabilities and habits acquired by man as a member of society."[5] It is clear from the definition that culture evolves and thrives within the society. Society creates culture and culture on the other hand shapes society. Culture has a social character. It is not an individual thing. Individuals experience and transmit culture uniquely, but culture transcends individual experiences. Individuals within a culture share an interactive, learned perspective on appropriate social behavior. Here culture includes the behavioral pattern of individuals within the society. In the words of Niebuhr:

> Individuals may use culture in their own ways; they may change elements in their culture, yet what they use and change is social. Culture is the social heritage they (individuals within society) receive and transmit. Whatever is purely private, so that it neither derives from nor enters into social life is not a part of culture. Conversely, social life is always cultural.[6]

Based on this understanding, Niebuhr, went ahead to define culture as that which "includes speech, education, tradition, myth, science, art, philosophy, government, law, rite, belief, inventions, technologies."[7]

As a people's way of life, culture, therefore, "Explicitly and implicitly teaches its members how to organize their experience. To learn a culture is to learn how to perceive, judge, and act in ways that are recognizable, predictable, and understandable to others in the same community."[8] Culture is not simply about behavior. It is also about ideas. The mental basis of culture is commonly stressed in modern definitions of culture. For example, Clifford Geertz defines culture as, "A system of inherited conceptions expressed in symbolic forms by means of which human beings communicate, perpetuate and develop their knowledge about, and their attitudes towards life."[9]

In traditional societies, there is a very close connection between religion and culture. In his attempt to portray the connection between religion and culture and how they can impact each other, Aylward Shorter said:

> Culture is essentially a transmitted pattern of meanings embodied in symbols, a pattern capable of development and change, and it belongs to the concept of humanness itself. It follows that, if religion is a human phenomenon or human activity, it must affect, and be affected by, culture.[10]

Religion can therefore be seen as part of a cultural system, and cannot exist independently or outside of a culture. Culture is the vehicle for the transmission of religion, just as religion is also a vehicle for the transmission of culture.

Having established a working definition of culture, we shall now proceed to attempt a definition of religion.

Religion: A Definition.

Like culture, the term religion lacks a precise definition. I may say that it easier to define culture than religion. Expressing this fact, Haught writes, "Literally thousands of scholars have attempted to define religion, always with less than satisfying results. No matter how carefully they "define" religion, other experts will eagerly indicate what the definition has left out."[11]

However, the difficulty not with standing, we shall try to find a definition for religion as a working tool for our research.

Tracing the derivation and definition of the term religion, the *New Advent Catholic Encyclopedia* states that:

> The derivation of the word "religion" has been a matter of dispute from ancient times. Not even today is it a closed question. Cicero, in his "De natura deorum", II, xxviii, derives religion from *relegere* (to treat carefully): "Those who carefully took in hand all things pertaining to the gods were called *religiosi*, from *relegere*." Max Muller favored this view. But as religion is an elementary notion long antedating the time of complicated ritual presupposed in this explanation, we must seek elsewhere

42

for its etymology. A far more likely derivation, one that suits the idea of religion in its simple beginning, is that given by Lactantius, in his "Divine Institutes", IV, xxviii. He derives religion from religare (to bind): "We are tied to God and bound to Him [*religati*] by the bond of Piety, and it is from this, and not, as Cicero holds, from careful consideration [*relegendo*], that religion has received its name."[12]

In this essay, we shall look more into definitions of religion that does not limit the concept of religion to a theistic frame of mind; definitions that explicitly do not understand religion as revolving around the idea of a God or gods, though implicitly do not deny that such concept is one of the essential elements of religion. Based on this understanding, religion can be defined as, "Humans being's relation to that which they consider as holy, sacred, spiritual, or divine."[13] That which humans regard as holy, sacred, spiritual or divine could be anything not limited to God or gods. In Judeo-Christian religion, and in other theistic religions, it could be God or gods, and other concepts like heaven, holy peoples, places, objects etc. In non-theistic religions like Buddhism, it could be Nirvana, the Tathagatha, the three Jewels, or even the arhats or bodhisattvas. In short, it could be different thing to different people and religion.

Moving further in this direction, Paul Tillich defined religion as "that which is of ultimate concern."[14] Such concerns could be problem the of suffering, life and death, relationship with the Ultimate Reality, man's final destiny, etc. Approaching religion from a sociological point of view, Emile Durkheim wrote, "Religion is unified system of beliefs and practices relative to sacred things, that is to say things set apart and forbidden – beliefs and practices which unites into one single moral community . . . all those who adhere to them."[15] On his part, Clifford Geertz identified religion among other things as a cultural system. In his understanding, religion is:

> A system of symbols which acts to establish powerful, pervasive, and long—lasting moods and motivations in men by formulating conceptions of a general order of existence and clothing these conceptions with such aura of factuality that the mood and motivations seem uniquely real.[16]

After a comprehensive analysis or study of World Religions, Lewis M. Hopfe and Mark R. Woodward came up with a broad description of religion that, one or way the other, tends to cover what various people have defined as religion or called religion. According to them, religion:

> (1) Usually, but not always, deal in some way with people's relationship to the unseen world of spirits, ancestors, gods, and demons; (2) they usually have developed a system of myths about the unseen world and rituals designed for communing with or propitiating the spirits (or whatever is considered the Ultimate); (3) they usually have developed a cult of organized rituals, temple (and other places of worship), priests, and scriptures at some point in history; (4) they usually have some statement about life beyond death, either as survival in some shadowy hades, in some version of heaven and hell, or through reincarnation; (5) they usually have developed a code of conduct or moral order; and (6) they generally have attracted large followings, either currently or at some time in the past.[17]

Religion is a universal phenomenon that encompasses all of human activities. It has been rightly said that, "Wherever people are found, there too is religion."[18] In fact, in most societies, like Islamic society, it is religion that regulates every activity from social, economic, political to marital life. The journey from life through death is religious.

The Marriage of Culture and Religion.

How does culture relate to religion, or put in another way, does culture generally influence religion? Yes. This is because every religious system (Judaism, Christianity, Confucianism, Hinduism, Buddhism, Islam, Taoism, Zoroastrianism, etc) is born within a cultural context. According to Hopfe and Woodward,

> For each religion, four major points are considered. (1) What culture produced this religion? (2) If there was a founder, and anything can be known of the founder's life, what factor caused this person to found this religion? (3) If there are scriptures or sacred texts, what do they tell us about this religion? (4) What have been the major historical developments of this religion?[19]

All these points revolve around the influence of culture on religion. For example, what are the socio-cultural background of the founder, and the worldview of his time? The socio-cultural background will influence the message and choice of words in the sacred text, and the historical developments are seen along the line of cultural epochs of the society. Taking Christianity and Jesus as an example, Jesus was born within the context of a particular culture, he grew within this culture, and he expressed and communicated his message within the cultural milieu. Put in the words of Shorter,

> There could have been no earthly ministry for Jesus if he had not adopted the cultural concepts, symbols and behavior of his hearers. His cultural solidarity with the Palestinian communities of his day was a necessary condition for communicating with them.[20]

As we cannot understand Jesus and his message or religion outside the cultural context of the 1st century B.C.E Palestine, so we cannot understand the Buddha and Buddhism outside the cultural context of India. This is true also of Islam and Muhammad. By extension also, we cannot understand the spread and impact of Buddhism in China outside the cultural influence of Chinese culture on Buddhism as a religion in China.

Culture as we have already seen is the totality of a people's way of life; their ethos and worldview, and we cannot imagine any religion coming up or taking root in any given society outside the people's way of life, their ethos and worldview. According to Geertz:

> In religious belief and practice a group's ethos is rendered intellectually reasonable by being shown to represent a way of life ideally adapted to the actual state of affair the world view describes . . . religious rituals, no matter how apparently automatic or conventional, involves the symbolic fusion of ethos and world view.[21]

In traditional societies, there is no dichotomy between religion and culture. Cultural performances are religious celebrations. Culture produces religion and at the same time culture is understood from the religious perspective. Describing the African religion and culture, with particular reference to the Igbo tribe in Nigeria, Ejizu said it, "Religion is the womb of culture in the traditional Igbo background. It permeates most aspects of life, and infuses them with meaning and significance."[22]

Having established that every religion is influenced by culture, Buddhism inclusive, the question then is: how did Chinese culture influence Buddhism in China?

The Influence of Culture on Buddhism in China.

Historically, Buddhism entered China through the Silk Road during the Han Dynasty. At this time Confucianism, Taoism, and Chinese indigenous cultural religions, were at their peak. Confucianism was the state religion, while Taoism was the popular religion. On their own part, Confucianism and Taoism were products of the Chinese cultural system. Reporting on this, Parrinder said,

> Confucianism and Taoism have been regarded as part
> of the collective cultural heritage of the Chinese . . . For

much of Chinese history, Confucianism and Taoism have been thought of by the Chinese themselves as manifestations *par excellence* of the national ethos, and not specifically as religious faith inviting conversion, membership and personal commitment.[23]

It is natural that when Buddhism came to China, it was influenced by the religio-cultural system that was already established. On this again, Parrinder reported, "So powerful was this indigenous traditional that, after the introduction of Buddhism to China, Buddhism became increasingly Chinese in character. Purely Chinese schools of Buddhism were born."[24] Prominent among these purely Chinese are the Tiantai, Chan (Zen), and Pure Land schools of Buddhism. Before Buddhism could make impact on the Chinese, it had first to become Sinicized, to become at home, to find a Chinese way of expressing itself. To achieve this, Buddhism has to be influenced and transformed by Chinese culture. Expressing this fact, Kenneth S. Ch'en said that:

> It is true that the process of Indianization of China through Buddhism did take place, but before this could take place, there was first the adaptation of Buddhism to Chinese conditions. The Chinese fashioned changes in the Indian ideas and practices, so that Buddhism became more and more Chinese and more acceptable to the Chinese . . . when Buddhism was introduced to China, the Chinese were not totally overwhelmed by the new religion. It is true that for few a centuries, the Chinese were captivated by the overpowering religious panorama brought in with Buddhism, but in time, what some scholars call the basic personality or local genius of the Chinese began manifesting itself. By this local genius or national character is meant the sum total of the cultural traits, which the vast majority of the Chinese adhered to, traits that had been developed by them during their long history. It was through the manifestation of this

local genius that they were able to choose ideas from the Indian religion and modify them to fit the Chinese religion.[25]

The above quotation clearly shows the influence of Chinese culture on the Buddhism.

This influence as we have mentioned are seen in the distinctive characteristics of Chinese Schools of Buddhism. To appreciate this fact, let us give some concrete instances of this influence.

First, there is the influence of Chinese language in Chinese Buddhism. For Buddhism to take root in China, the Indian ideas and concepts had to be interpreted and expressed in Chinese ideas and language. According to Wright,

> In these early efforts – in oral discourse, written translation, and exegesis – to present Buddhist ideas in Chinese language and metaphor, there was necessarily a heavy reliance on the terms and concepts of indigenous traditions. Buddhism somehow had to be "translated" into terms that Chinese could understand.[26]

The Chinese religio-cultural terms that were employed heavily influenced the teaching and understanding of Buddhism in China. For example:

> The Taoist term for immortals, *chen-jen*, served as a translation of the Buddhist word *Arhat*, "the fully enlightened one." *Wu-wei*, non-"action" was used to render the Buddhist term for ultimate release, *Nirvana*. The Confucian expression *Hsiao-shün*, "filial submission and obedience" was used to translate the general and abstract word *Śīla*, 'morality.'"[27]

This example suggests the subtle ways in which Buddhism was influenced by the Chinese culture, and was prepared and adapted for a Chinese audience through translations.

In China also the religio—cultural influence influenced Buddhism, originally a-theistic, to put on vestiges of a theistic religion. As expressed by Wright,

> Ultimately, Buddhist, Taoist, and folk religious elements fused into an almost undifferentiated popular religion. The pantheon was, in a sense, the victim of its own adaptability. It had been easy for a Buddha or a bodhisattva to take on one or more attributes of the local god and replace him in the temple of the local cult. But now, its original Buddhist character was gradually obliterated as the god took on other attributes given him by his devotees. This Sinicization of the Buddhist pantheon began at least as early as the Sung dynasty.[28]

Another area of Chinese cultural influence on Buddhism in China is the area of art and imagery. No sooner was Buddhism rooted in China than the Buddhist art and images were adapted to reflect Chinese cultural and artistic outlook. Wright, citing Alexander Soper, described some aspect of this process, "The [Chinese] artists transformed the bodhisattva type from a swart half-naked Indian to a more decently clad divinity with proper light complexion; the faithful gave special honor to the figure in the pantheon who claimed personal connection with China."[29] Such modifications are evident in the image and understanding of the bodhisattvas Avalokiteśvara and Maitreya. Commenting on the influence of Chinese culture on these two bodhisattvas in Chinese Buddhism, Ch'en wrote:

> There is no question that within Buddhist tradition Avalokiteśvara was regarded as male deity. With popular Buddhism (in China), however, there is a different tradition which presents the bodhisattva in the delicate, beautiful, and slender female so universally admired not only in East Asia but also throughout the art of the West. In this popular form the deity is commonly referred to

in the West as the Chinese Madonna, in the East as Sung-tzu, or kuan-yin, the Giver of children.[30]

This transition and transformation of Kuan-yin was not simply the making of Buddhism but rather the religio-cultural influence of China, especially the non-sectarian Chinese indigenous native religions that revere Kuan-yin as the venerable mother or the Eternal mother. Commenting also on Maitreya, Ch'en said:

> Maitreya likewise underwent a transformation in China. Very early in the Pāli tradition Maitreya appears as the future Buddha waiting to be reborn on earth to purify the religion in some distant future. In the meantime, he is the bodhisattva living in the Tushita Heaven. Overall, he does not play an important role in Indian Buddhism. Only after he was introduced into China did he become an important figure. By the fourth century A.D., there was a Maitreya cult in which the devotees vowed to be reborn in Tushita Heaven in order to see Maitreya face to face.[31]

It is clear from all the above instances that Chinese Buddhism as we see it today was heavily influenced by Chinese culture.

Conclusion.

In this essay, we have established the fact that every religion is born, develops, and thrives with a cultural system. In this birth and development, culture leaves a lasting influence on religion. The question that one may ask is: does the culture in which a particular religion is born or in which its takes root or is introduced, remain the same after the birth or the introduction of that religion? The answer is No. In other words, as culture influences religion, so does religion influence culture. This is very true also of Buddhism in China. Attesting to this fact, Yang I-fan, said:

Buddhism attained its first stage of development in China from the third to sixth century A.D. Its philosophy and teachings gradually merged with the Chinese culture . . . Buddhism influence many aspects of the daily life of the people and played an important part in the spiritual life of the nation.[32]

Lending his voice to that of Yang I-fang, Wright, said:

One of the great themes in the history of Eastern Asia is the transformation of Chinese culture by Buddhism. We can trace this process across nearly two millennia of time and we can see it at work in any aspect of Chinese life and thought.[33]

There is, therefore, such an intrinsic relationship between culture and Buddhism in China, and between religion and culture overall.

Notes.

1. John F. Haught, *What is Religion? An Introduction.* (New York: Paulist Press, 1990), 1.

2. Wilfred Cantwell Smith, *The Meaning and End of Religion.* (Minneapolis: Fortune Press, 1991), 53.

3. William Reese, *Dictionary of Philosophy and Religion.* (New York: Humanity Books, 1999), 151.

4. H. Richard Niebuhr, *Christ and Culture.* (New York: Harper and Row, 1951), 33.

5. Edward B. Tylor, *Primitive Culture.* (New York: J.P. Putnam & sons, 1920), 1.

6. Niebuhr, *Christ and Culture*, 33.

7. Ibid.

8. Duane E. Campbell, *Choosing Democracy: A practical guide to Multicultural Education, 3rd Ed.* (New Jersey: Prentice Hall, 2004), 43.

9. Clifford Geertz, *The Interpretation of Culture.* (New York: Basic Books, 1975), 89

10. Aylward Shorter, *Towards a Theology of Inculturation.* (New York: Orbis Books, 1997), 5.

11. Haught, *What is Religion? An Introduction*, 2.

12. Charles Francis Aiken, "Religion" *New Advent Catholic Encyclopedia.* Vol.12 (New York: Robert Appleton Company,)1911

13. The New Encyclopedia Britannica, Micropaedia, Ready Reference vol. 9. (Chicago: University of Chicago, 1990), 1016.

14. Paul Tillich, *The Protestant Era.* (Chicago: University of Chicago Press, 1948), 59.

15. Emile Durkheim, *The Elementary Forms of the Religious Life.* (New York: The Free Press, 1965), 62.

16. Geertz, *The Interpretation of Cultures*, 90.

17. Lewis M. Hopfe and Mark R. Woodward, *Religions of the World, 8th.* (New Jersey: Prentice Hall, 2001), 6.

18. Ibid.

19. Ibid.

20. Shorter, *Towards a Theology of Inculturation*, 80.

21. Geertz, *The Interpretation of Cultures*, 89-90, 113.

22. Christopher Ejizu, *The Influence of African Indigeneous Religions on Roman Catholicism, The Igbo Example.* http:// www.afrikaworld.net/afrel/ejizu-atrcath.htm (accessed May 18, 2008).

23. Geoffrey Parrinder, *World Religions from Ancient History to the Present.* (New York: Newness Books, 1983), 336

24. Ibid.

25. Kenneth S. Ch'en, *The Chinese Transformation of Buddhism.* (New Jersey: Princeton University Press, 1973), 5-6

26. Arthur F. Wright, *Buddhism in Chinese History.* (Stanford: Stanford University Press, 1959), 36.

27. Ibid.

28. Ibid, 98.

29. Ibid.

30. Ch'en, *The Chinese Transformation of Buddhism*, 6-7.
31. Ibid, 7-8.
32. Yang I-fan, *Buddhism in China.* (Hong Kong: Union Press, 1956), 2.
33. Wright, *Buddhism in Chinese History*, 1.

2.4 THE DEPARTURE OF CHINESE UNDERSTANDING OF BUDDHISM FROM THE VIEWS HELD IN INDIA.

When Buddhism travelled to China from India, it became sinicized. With this, there was a departure from the views held in India. Reporting on this, Parrinder said, "So powerful was the indigenous tradition that, after the introduction of Buddhism to China, Buddhism became increasingly Chinese in character. Purely Chinese schools of Buddhism were born."[1]

In India, Buddhist philosophy was otherworldly. This idea was change largely in China. The Buddhist monks became involved in the ownership and administration of property. Again, the Indian Buddhist idea of individualism changed in China because of the family centered Confucian Chinese society. In addition, the Indian non-theistic Buddhists understanding also changed in China. Here, Buddhism began to put on vestiges of a theistic religion.

There also a departure from Indian views in the area of translations. For Buddhism to take root in China, the Indian ideas would necessarily put on Chinese understanding. For example:

> The Taoist term for immortals, *chen-jen*, served as a translation of the Buddhist word *Arhat*, "the fully enlightened one." *Wu-wei*, non-"action" was used to render the Buddhist term for ultimate release, *Nirvana*. The Confucian expression *Hsiao-shün*, "filial submission and obedience" was used to translate the general and abstract word *Sīla*, 'morality.'"[2]

Another departure is seen in the area of arts and imagery. No sooner was Buddhism rooted in China than the Buddhist art and images were adapted to reflect Chinese understaning and artistic outlook. Alexander Soper, cited by Wright, described some aspect of this process, "The [Chinese] artists transformed the bodhisattva type from a swart half-naked Indian to a more decently (Chinese) clad divinity with proper light complexion."[3] Such modifications are evident in the images and understanding of the bodhisattvas Avalokiteśvara and Maitreya. Commenting on this, Ch'en wrote:

> There is no question that within Buddhist tradition Avalokiteśvara was regarded as male deity. With popular Buddhism (in China), however, there is a different tradition which presents the bodhisattva in the delicate, beautiful, and slender female figure as Sung-tzu, or kuan-yin, the Giver of children.[4]

Commenting also on Maitreya, Ch'en said:

> Maitreya likewise underwent a transformation in China. Very early in the Pāli tradition Maitreya appears as the future Buddha waiting to be reborn on earth to purify the religion in some distant future. On the whole he does not play an important role in Indian Buddhism. Only after he was introduced into China did he become an important figure. By the fourth century A.D., there was a Maitreya cult in which the devotees vowed to be reborn in Tushita Heaven in order to see Maitreya face to face.[5]

Chinese Buddhism developed a salvific type of Buddhism with an understanding that one can achieve salvation by relying upon the celestial Bodhisattvas and invoking the name of Amitabha. This is a shift from the Indian idea in which one attains enlightenment through personal efforts of practice and mediation.

Notes.
1. Geoffrey Parrinder, *World Religions from Ancient History to the Present.* (New York: Newness Books, 1983), 336.
2. Arthur F. Wright, *Buddhism in Chinese History.* (Stanford: Stanford University Press, 1959), 36.
3. Ibid.
4. Kenneth S. Ch'en, *The Chinese Transformation of Buddhism.* (New Jersey: Princeton University Press, 1973), 6-7.
5. Ibid, 7-8.

2.5 BUDDHISM IN THE HAN (CHINESE) DYNASTY

As it is impossible to discuss Buddhism and its spread in Indian without the Asokan Empire, so it is to discuss the Buddhist religion in China without the Han Dynasty; a Dynasty that saw to the official debut of Buddhism in China.

Under the Han Dynasty, Buddhism manifested strong intellectual characters in line with the philosophy of the empire. At this time, the major task was to translate the *Sutras* into Chinese language.

In addition to the intellectual characters, the Buddhism of the Han Dynasty was magical in nature. According to Harris Bell,

> The Buddhism that first became popular in China during the Han dynasty was deeply colored with magical practices, making it compatible with popular Chinese Taoism (a combination of folk beliefs and practices and philosophy). [1]

Again, a mixture of multi-religious practices characterized the Buddhism of this period. Its teachings and practices were not purely compatible with Buddhism as was practiced in India. According to Parrinder, it was "a Buddhism much modified by Taoist practices and adjusted to Indigenous ideas, which was acceptable among the Chinese people."[2]

Commenting on this, Bell said,

> Instead of the doctrine of no-self, early Chinese Buddhist taught the indestructibility of the soul. Nirvana became a kind of immorality . . . Until the end of the Han dynasty there was a virtual symbiosis between Taoism and Buddhism and a common propagation of the means for attaining immortality through various ascetic practices. It was widely believed that Lao-tzu, the founder of Taoism, had been reborn in India as Buddha. Many Chinese emperors worshiped Lao-tzu and the Buddha

on the same alter. The first transplantations of Buddhist sutras into Chinese – namely those dealing with such topics as breath control and mystical concentration – utilized a Taoist vocabulary to make Buddhist faith intelligible to the Chinese.[3]

While the Buddhism of the Han Dynasty was predominantly aristocratic and scholastic, the Jin Dynasty that followed was characterized by the popularization of Buddhism among the ordinary people.[4] This is not to say that the Buddhism of later Dynasties were devoid of the characteristics of the royal patronage that characterized the Han Dynasty. It is on record that,

> Apart from Emperor Ming in Han Dynasty, there were many emperors in China, who were great patrons in Buddhism, e.g. Emperor Wu in Lang Dynasty, Emperor Wu Ji-tian in Tang Dynasty. Buddhism was generally well-respected and supported by the emperors because it served as a moral framework for stability of the society.[5]

Generally, Buddhism in the China during the Han and later Dynasties manifested a double trend in character, "one was sophisticated and philosophical and the other was superstitious and religious. Moreover, like all other religions, Chinese Buddhism, during these dynasties, blended with other traditions and religions, which ultimately produced its own characteristics and features."[6]

Notes.
1. Harris Bell, *Buddhism in China*, http://www.globaled.org/curriculum/china/bessay1.htm (accessed July 7, 2008)
2. Geoffrey Parrinder, *World Religions: From Ancient History to the Present.* (New York: Facts on File, Inc.,1985), 346.
3. Bell, *Buddhism in China.* (assessed July 7, 2008)
4. *Han Buddhism*, Http://www.travelchinaguide.com/intro/religion/buddhism/han.htm (accessed July 7, 2008)

5. *Early Buddhism in China,* http://www.buddhistdoor.com/
OldWeb/bdoor/archive/nutshell/teach44.htm
(Accessed July 7, 2008)
6. Ibid.

CHAPTER THREE

ESSAYS ON CHRISTIANITY

3.1 CHRISTIANITY: BRIEF HISTORICAL FACTS.

Christianity originated in Palestine in about AD 33, with Jesus Christ as the founder. Christianity is a monotheistic religion with a Trinitarian dimension: Belief in One God in three persons – Father, Son, and Holy Spirit. It is the largest religion in the world with an estimated population of 2.2 billion adherents.

There are different traditions and groups within the Christian body. However, the religion is conveniently divided along two major traditions that emerged after the reformation era of the 16th Century: Catholicism and Protestantism.

Christianity has one central Scripture as its source of doctrines and teachings, namely the Bible, comprising the Old and New Testaments.

3.2 WHAT, IF ANYTHING, CAN THE STUDY OF COMPARATIVE RELIGION CONTRIBUTE TO MY UNDERSTANDING OF CHRISTIANITY?

Introduction.

As a growing Christian, one of the most interesting religious questions I have heard people asked is, will non-Christians be saved? The answer to this question was always in the negative. Such a negative answer came from the understanding of the Bible passage, "For of all the names in the world given to men, this (Jesus Christ) is the only name by which we can be saved."[1] Similar to this question was, as a believing Christian, am I supposed to fraternize with non-believing Christians? As usual, the answer was also in the negative, based on the Bible, which says, "Do not harness yourselves in an uneven team with unbelievers. Virtue is no companion for crime. Light and darkness have nothing in common. Christ is not the ally of Belial, nor has a believer anything to share with an unbeliever."[2] I grew up with this attitude of seeing people from other religions as miserable people without the hope of salvation, as darkness that, of necessity, needs the light of Christ, which comes by only converting to Christianity.

The study of Comparative Religion opened my eyes to realize how ignorant and blind I was in matters of religion and salvation, and how narrow I was in my understanding of the Christian teaching. How this study has affected and contributed to my better understanding of Christianity, is what I intend to discuss in this paper.

The Contributions of the Study of Comparative Religion to My Understanding of Christianity.

The study of Comparative Religion has contributed in no small way to my better understanding and practice of my religion as a Christian, not just as a Christian but as a Catholic Christian. Some of these contributions are:

i. **Christianity does not have the monopoly of truth:** I used to believe that my religion is the only true religion and possesses the whole truth of life. Through the study of Comparative Religion, I came to realize how wrong I was. Above all I came to understand that my religion needs other religions to see the TRUTH objectively and subjectively, in terms of faith. I came to appreciate the fact that no religion exists independent of the other. As expressed by Raimundo Panikkar[3] in his work *The Intrareligious Dialogue,* cited by Kessler, "Religions do not exist in isolation, but over against each other. There would be no Hindu consciousness were not for the fact of having to distinguish it from Muslims and Christians."[4] The truths I have come to learn from other religions through the Comparative Study of Religion have deepened the understanding of my faith. I have come to see the truth and beauty of other religions. To express this more clearly, I wish to borrow the words of Panikkar, with regard to my study of Comparative Religion; I began to realize that my neighbor's religion does not only challenge my own, but also enriches it. I began to realize that other religions possess the truth also. I began to accept that other religions may complement mine and in some particular cases may supplement some of my beliefs provided that my religiousness remains an undivided whole. I began to see all religions as teaching and seeking the TRUTH, though from different directions.[5]

Again, I began to read with a better understanding and appreciation of the teaching of Vatican II concerning other religions possessing the truth. Vatican II stated, "The Catholic Church rejects nothing that is true and holy in these religions. She regards with sincere reverence those ways of conduct and of life, those precepts and teachings which, though differing in many aspects from the ones she holds and sets forth, nonetheless often reflect a ray of that Truth which enlightens all men." [6]

ii. Openness and tolerance: I grew up with the famous sayings of St. Cyprian: 'Outside the Church, no salvation.' With this, I excluded people of all religions from being saved. The study of Comparative Religion changed this erroneous idea. It made me read with a new understanding the teachings of the Church enshrined in Vatican II Document, *Lumen Gentium* that says, those who have not yet received the Gospel are related in various ways to the people of God. In the first place we must recall the people to whom the testament and the promises were given and from whom Christ was born according to the flesh (the Jews). But the plan of salvation also includes those who acknowledge the Creator. In the first place amongst these there are the Muslims who, professing to hold the faith of Abraham, along with us adore the one and merciful God, who on the last day will judge mankind. Nor is God far distant from those who in shadows and images seek the unknown God. Those also can attain to salvation who through no fault of their own do not know the Gospel of Christ or His Church, yet sincerely seek God and moved by grace strive by their deeds to do His will as it is known to them through the dictates of conscience. Nor does Divine Providence deny the helps necessary for salvation to those who, without blame on their part, have not yet arrived at an explicit knowledge of God and with His grace strive to live a good life. Whatever good or truth is found amongst them is looked upon by the Church as a preparation for the Gospel.[7]

The study of Comparative Religion gave me a spirit of openness and tolerance realizing that God does exclude any one from salvation based on religious affiliations as clearly explained the teachings of Vatican II cited above. More importantly, my first time of staying together with Buddhist monks and nuns, the first time of entering a non Christian Church is within this study of Comparative Religion. This interaction has enriched my understanding and practice of my faith. I have become very tolerant and came to appreciate the beauty of religious diversity.

iii. A better reading and understanding of the Bible: The study of Comparative Religion has made me to understand that the Bible is not the only Sacred Scripture as I use to think. This knowledge made me to develop a keen interest in reading not just the Bible but other Scripture. I felt "enlightened" to discover that other scriptures are teaching the truth contained in the Bible, for example the GOLDEN RULE: "Always treat others as you would like them to treat you."[8] This I found reflected in other religions in these ways:

Islam: Not one of you truly believes until you wish for others what you wish for yourselves.[9]

Judaism: What is hateful to you, do not do to your neighbor. This is whole Torah; all the rest are commentary.[10]

Buddhism: Treat not others in ways that you yourself would find hurtful.[11]

Taoism: Regard you neighbor's gain as your own gain and your neighbor's loss as your own loss.[12]

Hinduism: This is the sum of duty: do not do to others what would cause pain if done to you.[13]

Jainism: One should treat all creatures in the world, as one would like to be treated.[14]

Zoroastrianism: Do not do unto others whatever is injurious to yourself.[15] Confucianism: One word which sums up the basis of all good conduct: Loving-kindness. Do not do to others what you do not want done to yourself.[16]

Sikhism: I am a stranger to no one; and no one is a stranger to me. Indeed, I am a friend to all.[17]

Conclusion.

I can go on and on to enumerate the various ways that the study of Comparative Religion has contributed to my better understanding and practice of Christianity, but the scope of this paper cannot accommodate it all. Suffice to say that I now have a better understanding of what it means to be religious in general and in particular to be a Christian. I have come to understand that religion is more than Christianity. I have come to see with an unbiased mind the rich varieties and grandeur of other religions of the world.

The study of Comparative Religion is a program I very much recommend to every religious person, especially those religious fundamentalists and dogmatists who are intoxicated and are suffocating in religious syncretism and dogmatism respectively.

Notes.
1. Acts. 4:12.
2. 2 Cor. 6: 14-15.

3. Raimundo Panikkar, *The Intrareligious Dialogue* (New York: Paulist Press. 1978) cited by Gary E. Kessler, *Philosophy of Religion*, 532-535.

4. Gary E. Kessler, *Philosophy of Religion: Towards a Global Perspective.* (California: Wadsworth Publishing Company, 1999), 535.

5. Ibid., 534-535.

6. Vat. II, *Nostra Aetate*, no. 2.

7. Vat. II, *Lumen Gentium*, no. 16.

8. Matt. 7:12.

9. *Muhammad's Hadith.*

10. *Hillel, Talmud, Shabbat* 31a.

11. The Buddha, *Udana – Varga* 5:18.

12. Lao Tzu, *T'ai Shang Kan Yin P'ien*, 213-218.

13. *Mahabharata* 5:1517.

14. Mahavira, *Sutrakritanga.*

15. *Shayast-na-Shayast* 13.29.

16. Confucius Analects 15.23.

17. *Guru Granth Sahib*, 1299.

3.3 THE ATTRIBUTES OF THE ABSOLUTE (PERFECT WISDOM) IN THE PRAJNAPARAMITA (A BUDDHIST SCRIPTURE) VIS-À-VIS THE ATTRIBUTES OF THE ABSOLUTE (GOD) IN THE JUDEO-CHRISTIAN BIBLE.

Introduction.

What do we mean when we talk of the attribute(s) of a thing? Is it the name, nature, or function of the thing that we are referring to? The English word *"Attribute"* has a Latin root. According to Reese, "attribute" is from the Latin *ad* ("to") and *tribuere* ("ascribe"). Hence, that which is ascribed to a thing.[1] In religious terms, it is used to refer to the essential characteristics of the Divine or the Ultimate. The use of word attribute in this essay refers, therefore, to the essential characteristics of the Perfect Wisdom as contained in the Prajnaparamita, and of God as contained in the Bible.

Is there any relationship between the attributes of the Perfect Wisdom as enshrined in this Buddhist sutra (Prajnaparamita) and the attributes of God as enshrined in the Judeo-Christian Holy Book (the Bible)? This question will be addressed in this essay.

A Brief Background of the Prajnaparamita and the Bible.

To put this essay in its proper context, we will begin with a brief background of the two sacred texts in Buddhist and Judeo-Christian traditions, which are the basis of our discussion. According to Conze, works on Prajnaparamita, "perfect wisdom," were composed by Indian Buddhists over a period of more than 1,000 years, between 100 B.C. and A.D.1100. Within Buddhism it inaugurated the emergence of the Mahayana and continued to guide its further development.[2] Describing the influence of the Prajnaparamita, Conze said that after the Torah, the Koran and the Gospels, the Indian literature of "The Perfection of Wisdom" has had the greatest impact on the religious consciousness of humankind. The work presented in "The Perfection of Wisdom in Eight Thousand Lines and its Verse Summary", were composed in South India.[3]

Like the Prajnaparamita, the Bible was written over a long period. It covers the period of what we now called the Old and

New Testament eras, and so is divided accordingly into the Old Testament and the New Testament. According to Ringer, the Old Testament books were written 1450-400 B.C. The New Testament books were written 45-95 A.D.[4] The Bible is believed by both Jews and Christians to be the true Word of God. In the words of Broderick "The Bible is the inspired word of God written under inspiration of the Holy Spirit and gathered in the order of the providence of God."[5]

The Attributes of the Absolute (Perfect Wisdom) in the Prajnaparamita.

The Absolute has five identifiable attributes namely: it is unthinkable, incomparable, immeasurable, incalculable, and equals the unequalled. These attributes were made known in the conversation between *Subhuti* and *The Lord Buddha*. It written thus:

> *Subhuti:* Deep, O Lord is prefect wisdom. Certainly as a great enterprise has this perfection of wisdom been set up, as an unthinkable, incomparable, immeasurable, incalculable enterprise, as an enterprise which equals the unequalled.

> *The Lord:* So it is . . . In like manner also all dharmas are unthinkable, incomparable, immeasurable, incalculable, and equal to the unequalled.[6]

These attributes will be explained one by one.

i. Unthinkable: The Absolute (Perfect Wisdom) is beyond human comprehension and rationality. It is unimaginable. As the *Lord* put it, why is it unthinkable enterprise? Because unthinkable are Tathagatahood, Buddhahood, Self-existence, and the state of all-knowledge. And on these no one can reflect with one's thoughts! How impossible to count them. I could no more count them than I could the dharmas which constitute thought. They are unthinkable because all thought has ceased.[7]

ii. Incomparable: The Absolute cannot be compared with anything because it is above everything, and cannot be reflected upon. There is nothing like it. According to the *Lord*, no one cannot reflect on Tathagatahood, nor compare it. The Tathagata-dharmas are incomparable because they have completely risen above all comparison.[8] They cannot be placed side by side with anything, and that is why they cannot be compared.

iii. Immeasurable: The Absolute cannot be measured because it is beyond thought; it is infinite, void, sign-less, and wishes-less, not produced, not stopped and non-existent. This is expressed very clearly in the Prajnaparamita, "One cannot conceive the measure of a form since such a measure does not exist, in consequence of the infinitude of all dharmas . . . For all dharmas are empty in their own-being; they have no individuality, no personality, they are like an illusion, a dream, an echo, a reflect image."[9]

iv. Incalculable: Since the Absolute has no form, is empty and is like an illusion, it cannot be counted. It is unquantifiable. In the words of the *Lord*, it cannot be counted because it has arisen above possibility of counting.[10]

v. Equal to the Unequalled: This means that the Absolute is truly the absolutely

Absolute beyond whom there is nothing. It unequalled everything and cannot share equally with anything. As expressed in the Prajnaparamita, "nothing can be equal to the Tathagatahood, to the fully Enlightened one, to the Self-existent, to the All-knowing, how much less can anything be superior to him?"[11]

The Attributes of Absolute (God) in the Bible.

I wish to point out that my concern here is not to discuss all the attributes of God in the Bible but to see how the five attributes of the Absolute in the Prajnaparamita are reflected as the attributes of God in the Bible. All the five attributes of the Perfect Wisdom (unthinkable, incomparable, immeasurable, incalculable, and equals the unequalled) are also attributes of God in the Bible. I will also take them one by one.

i. God is Unthinkable: The nature of God is beyond human comprehension and rationality. His ways are too deep for human thinking, they are unsearchable and unfathomable. The Bible says, "Who can claim to grasp the mystery of God, to understand the perfection of the Almighty? It is higher than the heavens . . . It is deeper than Sheol: what can you know?"[12]

ii. God is Incomparable: He incomparable with anything. He is above everything in everything. In the book of Exodus, the Bible says "Who among the gods is like you, O Lord? Who is your like, majestic in holiness, terrible in deeds of prowess, worker of wonder?"[13] Again the Psalmist puts it this way, "There is none to compare with you, no achievement to compare with yours."[14]

iii. God is Immeasurable: Even though God is expressed in human terms, He is

Infinite, He is a Spirit.[15] He cannot be measure because He is a spiritual being. He is empty, void, and has no measurable properties. As expressed in the Psalms, "Great is the Lord, and greatly to be praised. His greatness is beyond measure."[16]

iv. God is Incalculable: Like the Perfect wisdom, God is uncountable and unquantifiable. It is written in the Psalms "God how hard is it to grasp your thoughts! How impossible to count them. I could no more count them than I could the sand."[17] As it is impossible to count the sand of the earth, so is God incalculable.

v. God is Equal to the Unequalled: He is Sovereign, Almighty,

Omnipotent, Omniscient, and above all. He is equal to nothing, He is Supreme, and He is Absolute. In the Bible, God said to Abraham, "I am El Shaddai."[18] *El Shaddai* is a Hebrew word meaning Almighty God. The book of Revelation says, "Alleluia! The Lord our God Almighty reigns."[19] He truly has no equal; He equals the unequalled.

Conclusion.

It is quite revealing how the teachings of the Prajnaparamita and Bible came to almost perfectly agree on the attributes of the Absolute as contained in both two sets of Holy books. It is evident that no religion has a monopoly on the truth. What is found in one religion can also be present in other religions, even though expressed differently, probably because of the language and culture from which the religion emerged.

Although the attributes of the Absolute (Perfect Wisdom) contained in the Prajnaparamita are expressed in the Bible, their understanding are not the same. In the Bible, the Absolute is a personal God, conceived as having the properties of a living being, with individuality and personality. He has a changeless existence; the same yesterday, today and tomorrow. In the Prajnaparamita, it is the opposite. The Perfect Wisdom does not have the properties of a living being, no individuality, no personality; it is impermanent. It is empty, devoid of all characterizations.[20]

Notes.

1. William L. Reese, *Dictionary of Philosophy and Religion*. (New York:
Humanity Books, 1999), 50.
2. Edward Conze, *The Ontology of the Prajnaparamita: Philosophy East and West*. (Hawaii: c. University of Hawaii Press, Vol. 3, 1953), 117.
3. Edward Conze, *The Perfection of Wisdom in Eight Thousand Lines and it*
Verse Summary. (India: Sri Satguru Publications, 1973), i.
4. Wesley Ringer, "History of the Bible: How the Bible Came to Us, in *GodAndScience.org* http://godandscience.org/apologetics/bibleorigin.html
(accessed on September 20, 2007).
5. Robert C. Broderick, *The Catholic Encyclopedia*. (New York: Thomas Nelson Publishers, 1976), 73.
6. Edward Conze, The Perfection of Wisdom, 181.
7. Ibid., 180-181.
8. Ibid.
9. Ibid., 181,278.
10. Ibid., 180.

11. Ibid.
12. Job 11:7
13. Exodus 15:11
14. Psalm 86:8
15. John 4:24
16. Psalm 145:3
17. Psalm 139:17-18
18. Genesis 17:1
19. Revelation 19:6
20. Edward Conze, *The Perfection of Wisdom*, 278.

3.4 THE EVIL OF PRIDE IN THE PRAJNAPARAMITA AND THE HOLY TEACHING OF VIMALAKIRTI (BUDDHIST SUTRA) AS REFLECTED IN THE JUDEO-CHRISTIAN SCRIPTURES.

Introduction.

Pride, especially in its negative form, is considered an evil to be avoided in all religions of the world if one is to have union with the Ultimate Reality, be it in the form of salvation, liberation, nirvana, enlightenment, etc., depending on one's religious affiliation. A brief look into the scriptures of some of the World Religions[1] will illustrate this point. In Judeo-Christian Scripture, pride is abhorrent to God, and brings the fall of man.[2] It is written in the Islamic Quran, "And do not swell your cheek (for Pride) at men, nor walk in insolence through the earth; for Allah does not love any arrogant boaster."[3] The Buddhist Diamond Sutra states that a proud person cannot achieve perfective enlightenment.[4] The Hindu Bhagavad-Gita states, "Those who know truly are free from pride and deceit."[5] In Jainism, pride brings more karma. It is written, "Not knowing the consequence of good and evil karmas, he is afflicted and hurt. Nevertheless, he, due to his egotism, piles up [more] karmas and undergoes births and deaths again and again."[6] The Shinto text says, "If you desire to obtain help, put away pride. Even a hair of pride shuts you off, as if by a great cloud."[7] Finally, Sikhism puts it this way, "The mightily proud ultimately rot in their own arrogance."[8] All these sacred texts portray the evil of pride in the scriptures of most religions of the world.

However, this essay is limited to the evil of pride in the Buddhist Mahayana Sutras: the Prajnaparamita and the Holy Teaching of Vimalakirti, as reflected in the Judeo-Christian Scripture – the Bible.

A Brief Insight into Our Texts.

To put our subject in context, it is necessary to give a brief background insight into our texts namely: the Prajnaparamita, the Vimalakirti, and the Bible.

The Prajnaparamita is considered the "Mother Sutra." According to Conze, Indian Buddhists composed segments of the Prajnaparamita over a period of more than 1,000 years, between 100 B.C. and 1100 A.D. Within Buddhism it inaugurated the emergence of the Mahayana and continued to guide its further development.[9] Describing the influence of the Prajnaparamita, Conze said that after the Torah, the Koran and the Gospels, the Indian literature of *The Perfection of Wisdom* has had the greatest impact on the religious consciousness of humankind. The work presented in "The Perfection of Wisdom in Eight Thousand Lines and its Verse Summary", was composed in India.[10]

The Holy Teaching of Vimalakirti is one of the oldest Mahayana scriptures. It was written at the time of the Buddha's earthly existence. According to Robert Thurman, "Nothing concrete is known about the "original text" of the Vimalakirti. It purports to record events that took place during the Buddha's time (sixth to fifth century B.C.). However, no text was apparent in India until after Nagarjuna (c. first century B.C. to first century A.D.) had revived the Mahayana traditions, discovering the Mahayana Sanskrit Scriptures (the *Vimalakirti* text among them).[11] Because of its beauty and uniqueness in presenting the Mahayana doctrine, the Vimalakirti has immense popularity among the Mahayana tradition of Buddhism. Accordingly, called 'jewel of Mahayana Sutra', this book presents the major teachings of Mahayana Buddhism in a precise and even harmonious form.[12] As implied by the title, the protagonist of this *Teaching of Vimalakirti* is a layman by the name of Vimalakirti, well-versed in the profundities of Mahayana Buddhism. The work has considerable appeal due to its dramatic contents, and is an important key to an understanding of the profound thought of Mahayana Buddhism.[13]

The Judeo-Christian Scripture is generally and commonly called the Bible. The term Bible in Latin and Greek is *biblia*, which literally means "the books." According to McKenzie, "The name 'the books' without qualification indicates the special position which these books occupied, and also shows that the Bible is a collection or a library rather than a single literary composition. The books of the Bible are called "sacred," because they are written under divine inspiration."[14] The Bible is divided into two major parts: the Old Testament, representing mainly the Jewish canon, but also used by Christians, and the New Testament, representing the Christian canon and used only by Christians. The Bible was written over a long period of time. According to Ringer, the Old Testament books were written 1450-400 B.C. The New Testament books were written 45-95 A.D.[15]

All these sacred texts mentioned above consider pride as evil.

What Is Pride?

Pride can be positive or negative. Our concern here is on negative pride. Various terms are used to describe the word pride words like arrogance, conceit, boastfulness, egotism, exaltedness, and haughtiness. Understanding what pride is will help us to better understand the context in which these terms are used in the Prajnaparamita, the Vimalakirti, and the Bible.

Pride is a feeling of self-importance, glorification, ascribing to oneself what one is not, or taking unto oneself the glory of another. It is exaggerating one's worthwhile looking down on others as less important or as less holy within the religious circle. It is self-righteousness. In its negative sense, pride is defined as "arrogant or disdainful conduct or treatment; haughtiness; an excessively high opinion of oneself; conceit. As in Christianity, Buddhism sees pride *(mana)* or conceit as something to be uprooted."[16]. As already mentioned above, no religion sees pride as a virtue. It is always seen as a vice that hinders a very devoted person from realizing his spiritual goal, and so must be avoided. Within this context, "Christianity considers pride to be one of the 'Seven Deadly Sins' and in Buddhism, it is one of the 'Ten Fetters.' The Ten Fetters are considered things that stand in the way of enlightenment and keep us stuck in the suffering cyclic existence.[17] Negative pride is characterized by a haughty attitude or a feeling of superiority, while devaluating others. It is considered problematic in Buddhism and Christianity. It is a type of arrogance whereby the person unjustifiably feels he is better than others. From the Buddhist perspective, this not only reinforces the wrong view that we are separate and distinct from others, but that we are somehow also superior.[18]

According to Nagarjuna, pride has seven forms:

◊ Boasting that one is lower than the lowly, or equal with the equal, or greater than or equal to the lowly, is called the pride of selfhood.

◊ Boasting that one is equal to those who by some quality are better than oneself is the pride of being superior.

◊ Thinking that one is higher than the extremely high, who fancy themselves superior, is the pride greater than pride; like an abscess in a tumor, it is very vicious.

◊ Conceiving an "I" through ignorance in the five empty aggregates, which are called the appropriation, is prideful.

◊ Thinking one has won fruits not yet attained is pride of conceit.

◊ Praising oneself for faulty deeds is known by the wise as wrongful pride.

◊ Deriding oneself, thinking 'I am senseless,' is called the pride of lowliness. Such are the seven prides.[19]

The Evil of Pride in the Prajnaparamita.

In the Prajnaparamita, pride is one of the deeds of Mara (the Evil One), and the Bodhisattva who is proud is said to be possessed by Mara. In his discussion with Subhuti, the Lord said:

> But when there arises in him the conceit, 'I have been predestined because by my declaration of the Truth manifold things get accomplished,' when a Bodhisattva sets him above other Bodhisattvas as one who has predestined, one should know that he stands in conceit, and has little intelligence. Again, as to the power of the name, Mara, having approached, will say to him: 'This is your name . . . when you are a Buddha, this will then be your name!' If he is one who has behaved in accordance with the ascetic practices, a devoted Yogin, Mara will tell him: 'Formerly in your past lives you have also had

these same qualities.' The Bodhisattva who, on hearing this, becomes conceited, one should know him to be possessed by Mara, of little intelligence.[20]

Possessed by Mara, full of pride, the Bodhisattva exalts himself. When there is pride, there is no detachment even though the Bodhisattva lives in the forest. Pride renders all his practices invalid. The Lord said, "The Bodhisattva who exalts himself, who depreciates others, one should know him to be possessed by Mara . . . Though he may reside in mountain caves, five hundred miles wide, infested with wild beasts, for many kotis of years: that Bodhisattva does not know this true detachment if he dwells contaminated by conceit."[21] Pride deprives the Bodhisattva of the Buddha cognition and enlightenment. The Prajnaparamita puts it this way, "Pride, arrogance, hauteur, false pride, conceit keep him away from all-knowledge, from the supreme cognition of a Buddha, from the cognition of the Self-Existent, from the cognition of the all-knowing, from supreme enlightenment. When he meets with Bodhisattvas who could be his good friends – virtuous in character, resolutely intent on the sublime, skilled in means, endowed with the irreversible dharma,—in his conceit he despises them, does not tend, love and honor them. So he will tighten the bond of Mara still further."[22]

The evil of pride is viewed with such consternation in the Prajnaparamita that it is seen as more serious that the four unforgiving sins, and the five deadly sins. The Prajnaparamita stated thus, "So serious is the offence of conceitedness . . . More serious than those four unforgivable offences is this production of a proud thought, when on the occasion of the prediction of his name, a Bodhisattva has despised other Bodhisattvas, and produced a thought which is very unwholesome, which is more serious than the four unforgiveable offences. Not only that, but it is more serious even than the five deadly sins, this production of a thought connected with pride."[23]

Such is the magnitude of the evil of pride in the Prajnaparamita.

The Evil of Pride in the Holy Teaching of Vimalakirti.

The Vimalakirti sees pride as a vice, which must be avoided if the Bodhisattva is to attain the Buddha qualities. The protagonist, Vimalakirti, achieved great honor by not being proud, but by acting in humility. It is said of him, "At that time, there lived in the great city of Vaisali a certain Licchavi, Vimalakirti by name. Having served the ancient Buddhas . . . he was honored as the aristocrat among aristocrats because he suppressed pride, vanity, and arrogance."[24]

In the Vimalakirti, there is no pride in the Buddha; he lived in humility so that living beings may not be proud but like him, might become humble. Responding to Reverend Ananda, Vimalakirti said, "Nevertheless since the Buddha has appeared during the time of the five corruptions, he disciplines living beings by acting lowly and humble."[25] Affirming what Vimalakirti said about the Buddha, Bukkyo said, "One of the eight virtues that enable Buddha to bestow blessings and happiness upon people is the ability to avoid pride and boasting."[26]

A Bodhisattva living in pride is following the wrong way and cannot attain the qualities of the Buddha. Addressing the question of Manjusri on the right way the Bodhisattva should follow to attain the qualities of the Buddha, Vimalakirti said, "When he goes into the states of the asuras, he remains free of pride, conceit, and arrogance."[27]

Pride excludes the Bodhisattva from communion with the Buddha, the Dharma, and the Sangha. Responding to the question of the goddesses on what joy in the pleasures of the Dharma is, Vimalakirti said, "It is the joy of unbreakable faith in the Buddha, of wishing to hear the Dharma, of observing the Sangha and honoring the spiritual benefactors without pride."[28] It is in the absence of pride, consummated in becoming the slave and the disciple of all living beings (humility) that one can practice and make the Dharma-sacrifice, which consists of heroic strength.[29]

In the Vimalakirti, a proud person cannot attain liberation and enlightenment. This is because he thinks he has something, whereas liberation consists in the emptiness of the Dharma. This is expressed thus, "Liberation is freedom from desire, hatred, and folly – that is the teaching for the excessively proud. However, those free of pride are taught that the very nature of desire, hatred, and folly is itself liberation. Whoever thinks, "I have attained! I have realized! is overly proud in the discipline of the well taught Dharma."[30]

It is in humility, not in pride, conceit, and arrogance that the Bodhisattva expresses his compassion and love for all living beings.

The Evil of Pride in the Judeo-Christian Scriptures.

In the Bible, various Hebrew and Greek words are used to express the term pride. The Hebrew words used in the Old Testament are: *geah, gaavah* – "proud, haughty"; *zed, zadon* – "pride, presumption." The Greek words used in the New Testament are: *hyperephania* – "to appear above, high"; *kauchema, kauchaomai* – "to boast"; *alazon, alazoneia* – "to boast"; *doxa* – "to glory."[31]

Looking at pride from the Judeo-Christian perspective, Broderick defined it as, "The chief of the capital sins, pride prompts and is partially present in all other sins. It is the inordinate desire for honor, recognition, and distinction. Pride arises from self-love. It is mortally sinful when it causes one to refuse to be subordinate even to God; it is less sinful if one though submissive, still seeks inordinately for honor."[32] In the Bible, the sin of pride is the sin of sins. It was this sin that transformed Lucifer, an anointed cherub of God, the very 'seal of perfection, full of wisdom and perfect in beauty,' into Satan, the devil, the father of lies, the one for whom Hell itself was created. St. Augustine described pride as the commencement of all sin.[33]

Pride hinders spiritual progress. It is hateful to God and to man. It is punishable by God, and must be overcome by Jews and Christians. The following Bible passages illustrate this point: Lev. 26:19, "And I will break the pride of your power." Prov. 6:16, "Pride is among the six things that God hates." Prov. 8:13, "I hate pride and arrogance." Ezekiel 28:11, 17, "You were once an exemplar of perfection, full of wisdom, perfect in beauty. Your heart has grown swollen with pride because of your beauty. You have corrupted your wisdom owing to your splendor." These are only few examples from the Old Testament.

The New Testament has the following examples: Matt. 23: 12, "Whoever shall exalt himself shall be abased." 2 Tim. 3:2, "For men shall be lovers of their own selves, covetous, boasters, proud, blasphemers, disobedient to parents, unthankful, unholy." James 4:6, "God resists the proud, but gives grace to the humble." Phil. 2:3, "With humility of mind let each regard one another as more important than himself. Look out for the interests of others." Speaking of Jesus, the Bible said, "His state was divine, yet he did not cling to his equality with God, but he emptied himself to assume the conditions of a slave. He was humbler yet, even to accepting death, death on a cross."[34] Jesus was never a proud man, but an embodiment of humility, and required his followers to be like him. He said, "Learn from me for I am meek and humble of heart, and you will find rest for your soul."[35]

From the above passages, it is obvious that both Judaism and Christianity treat pride with disdain.

Conclusion: A Synthesis of the Evil of Pride in the Prajnaparamita, Vimalakirti, and Judeo-Christian Scriptures.

In the Prajnaparamita, pride is seen as one of the deeds of Mara. It is more serious than the four unforgivable sins and the five deadly sins. In the Vimalakirti, although pride is associated with Mara, Mara is not directly the cause of pride. In the Bible, like in Prajnaparamita, pride is one of the six things God hates, and one of the seven he considers abominable. (cf. Prov. 6:16-17) Although pride is associated with the Devil in the Bible, he is not the cause of pride. He is a victim of pride as human beings are.

A very clear agreement between the three sacred texts on pride is that the proud person cannot attain salvation, liberation or enlightenment. The proud person has an over exaggerated importance of himself and despises other. Because of that he is thrown down, but the humble shall be liberated, rewarded and exalted.

Again, the Buddha, as portrayed in the Vimalakirti, during his earthly life acted lowly and in humility in his teachings and actions.

Similarly, the Bible portrayed Jesus as the embodiment and model of humility. Their followers are required to imitate them.

In sum, the three texts see pride as an evil that adherents must strive to avoid in order to attain perfection, liberation, enlightenment, and salvation.

Notes.

1. References of World Scriptures cited below are not directly from original texts. They are taken from *World Scripture; Pride and Egoism* http://www.unification.net/ws/theme051. htm_(accessed October 19, 2007)

2. Prov. 16: 5, 18

3. Surah 31: 18

4. *Diamond Sutra* 9.

5. Bhagavad-Gita 13;7

6. Acarangasutra 2. 55-56

7. Oracle of Kasunga

8. Adi Granth, *Gauri Sukhmani* 12, M.5, 278

9. Edward Conze, *The Ontology of the Prajnaparamita: Philosophy East and West.*

(Hawaii: c. University of Hawaii Press, Vol. 3, 1953), 117.

10 Edward Conze, *The Perfection of Wisdom in Eight Thousand Lines and its*

Verse Summary, (India: Sri Satguru Publications, 1973), i.

11. Robert A. F. Thurman, *The Holy Teaching of Vimalakirti.* (Pennsylvania: The Pennsylvania State University Press, 1976), ix

12. "The Holy Teaching of Vimalakirti," *Pennsylvania State University Website*, http://www.psupress.psu.edu/books/ titles/0-271-00601-3.html (accessed October 4, 2007).

13. Bukkyo Dendo Kyokai, *An Introduction to the Buddhist Canon.*_(Japan: Kenkysha printing Co.,1984), 60.

14. John L. Mckenzie, *Dictionary of the Bible.* (New York: Macmillan Publishing Co., Inc., 1965), 96.

15. Wesley Ringer, "History of the Bible: How the Bible Came to Us, in

GodAndScience.org   http://godandscience.org/apologetics/
   bibleorigin.html
(accessed on September 20, 2007).

16. "The Seven Deadly Sins of Buddhism," *About.com:Buddhism*
    http://buddhiam.about.com/od/keyconcepts/apride.
    htm?p=1 (accessed October 19,
2007)

17. "Pride – One of the Ten Fetters," *Prime Buddhist Center Website*
    *h*ttp://www.rimecenter.org/dharma.cfm?dharmaID=18
    (accessed October 19,
2007)

18. Ibid.

19. Nagarjuna, *Precious Garland*, 406-12

20. Conze, *Perfection of Wisdom*, 49

21. Ibid., 49-50

22. Ibid., 230

23. Ibid., 232-233

24. Thurman, *The Holy Teaching of Vimalakirti*, 20-21

25. Ibid., 33

26. Bukkyo Dendo Kyokai, *The Teaching of the Buddha*. (Japan:
    Kosaido Printing Co. Ltd., 1966), 38

27. Thurman, *The Holy Teaching of Vimalakirti*, 64

28. Ibid., 38

29. Ibid., 40

30. Ibid., 60

31. James A. Fowler, "Pride. An Outline Study of what the Bible
    says about pride." http://www.christinyou.net/pages/pride.
    html (accessed October 19, 2007)

32. Robert C. Broderick, *The Catholic Encyclopedia* (New York:
    Thomas Nelson
Publishers, 1976), 490-491

33. Phil. 2:6-8

34. "Sin of Pride – Sin of Self." http://www.AboutGOD.com/
    self-of-pride.htm (accessed October 19, 2007)

35. Matt. 11:28-30

3.5 LOVE AND COMPASSION IN THE HOLY TEACHING OF VIMALAKIRTI (BUDDHIST SUTRA) AS REFLECTED IN THE NEW TESTAMENT (CHRISTIAN BIBLE).

Introduction.

This essay deals with a comparative analysis of the concept of love and compassion as contained in the Buddhist Sutra, *The Holy Teaching of Vimalakirti*, and the Christian *New Testament Bible*. To discuss this, I will begin with a brief background of the two sets of holy books under consideration. This background analysis will help us understand the place of love and compassion, as a central theme, in these sacred texts. This essay will conclude with a synthesis of these concepts in the two texts.

A Brief Background of the Holy Teaching of Vimalarkirti and the New Testament.

The Holy Teaching of Vimalakirti is reputed to be one of the oldest Mahayana scriptures. It was written at the time of the Buddha's earthly existence. According to Robert Thurman, "Nothing concrete is known about the original text of the Vimalakirti. It purports to records of events that took place during Gautama Buddha's time (sixth to fifth century B.C.), but no text was apparent in India until after Nagarjuna (c. first century B.C. to first century A.D.) had revived the Mahayana traditions, discovering the Mahayana Sanskrit Scriptures, the Vimalakirti text among them."[1] Because of its beauty and uniqueness in presenting the Mahayana doctrine, the Vimalakirti has immense popularity among Mahayana Buddhists. Accordingly, "called 'jewel of Mahayana Sutras', this book presents the major teachings of Mahayana Buddhism in a precise and even harmonious form.[2] One these central teachings is love and compassion.

In this work, the lay teacher, Vimalakirti, becomes because sentient beings are ill. His compassion identifies totally with their suffering, and he will not rest or recover until they are liberated into freedom and peace.[3]

The New Testament occupies a place of primary importance in the lives of Christians. It is to taken to be the words of Jesus and or his immediate disciples. The New Testament is, "the name given to the final portion of the Christian Bible written after the Old Testament. Various unknown authors wrote the original texts after c. AD 45 and before c. AD 140. Its 27 books were gradually collected into a single volume over a period of several centuries.[4] Love and compassion is very much emphasized in the New Testament.

Love and Compassion in the Holy Teaching of the Vimalakirti

Compassion (*karuna*) expressed in love is the central teaching of the Vimalakirti. Compassion here is different from pity. It is not a feeling for someone, but rather a feeling with someone. It was in this feeling with the sufferings of living beings that Vimalakirti became sick, and will not recover until living beings recover. When asked by Manjusri the source of his sickness, Vimalakirti replied,

> Manjusri, my sickness comes from ignorance, and the thirst for existence, and it will last as long as do the sicknesses of all living beings . . . Were all living beings to be free from sickness, the bodhisattva also would be free from sickness. For example, Manjusri, when the only son of a merchant is sick, both parents become sick because of the sickness of their son. And the parents will suffer as long as that only son does not recover from his sickness. Just so, Manjusri, the bodhisattva loves all living beings as if each were his only child. He becomes sick when they are sick and is cured when they are cured. You ask me Manjusri, whence comes my sickness; the sickness of the bodhisattvas arise from great compassion.[5]

In response to Manjusri's question on how the bodhisattva generates great love toward all, Vimalakirti said, he generates love that is a refuge for all; love that is peaceful, free of passion, accords with reality, nondual. He generates the love that is great compassion because it infuses the Mahayana with radiance; the love that is never exhausted because it acknowledges voidness and selflessness; love that is tolerance, wisdom, liberative, and morality; love that is happiness because it introduces living beings to the happiness of the Buddha.[6]

The love and compassion of the Bodhisattva is a just a shadow of the love and compassion of the Buddha who is full of love and compassion. The Buddha told Ananda that great love and great compassion are special qualities of the Buddhas.[7] Vimalakirti expressed it this way: "Friends, the body of a Tathagata is the body of Dharma; it is born of love, compassion . . . the Buddha's causes living beings to awaken from their sleep, with the love that is spontaneous because it is fully enlightened."[8] In line with this, the Srimala Devi Sutra, said the love and compassion of the Tathagata is great and unlimited, bringing great and unlimited peace and comfort to the world.[9] Explaining further on the greatness of the Buddha's love and compassion, Kyokai said, "The spirit of Buddha is that of great loving kindness and compassion. The great compassion is the spirit that prompts it to be ill with illness of people, to suffer with their suffering."[10]

In sum, love and compassion is the basis of achieving enlightenment or nirvana.

Love and Compassion in the New Testament.

The whole of the New Testament is a gospel of God's love and compassion for humanity made manifest in and through Jesus. According to Leon-Dufour, "In the NT, divine love is expressed in a unique fact: Jesus came to live as God and as man, the dramatic dialogue of love between God and man.. .By his very existence, Jesus is the concrete revelation of love; Jesus fulfills the filial dialogue with God and bears witness of it to men. Jesus is God who comes to live out his love in the fullness of humanity and who came to make us understand the ardent appeal of love. In his very person man loves God and is loved by Him."[11] The New Testament clearly expressed this loving concern of God and His desire to free mankind from sin and suffering in the following words, "Yes, God loved the world so much that he gave his only son.. .For God sent his Sin into the world not to condemn the world, but so that through him the world might be saved."[12]

Compassion in the New Testament is more than pity. It is feeling with the sufferings of those who suffer. Compassion leads to salvation and not just temporary relief from pain. According to the Week of Compassion, "The New Testament word group frequently translated as "compassion," "compassionate," "to have compassion" has a theological focus that distinguishes it from the ordinary terms for "pity," "sympathy," and "mercy" frequently used to describe God's mercy as well as human feelings of tender concern. This "compassion" is more than a feeling. It is the New Testament word for God's saving, eschatological compassion as that compassion comes to expression in the person of Jesus."[13] In his ministry and action Jesus identified with the suffering, the sick, the lonely, the afflicted, the outcast, and the bereaved. The Bible described these actions in many moving ways: He was filled with compassion, he had great compassion, he was moved with compassion, and I have compassion.[14]

Love and compassion are not limited to Jesus alone; his disciples must imitate and follow his examples of love and compassion to all without exception and boundary. He said to them, "Be compassionate as your Father is compassionate."[15] To love in the New Testament is not optional, it is a command. Jesus again said to his disciples, "I give you a new commandment: love one another as I have loved you. By this love you have for one another, everyone will know that you are my disciples."[16] In the New Testament, love and compassion are the basis for salvation: eternal life or eternal damnation. Jesus implied this when he said, "He will say to those on his right, come and inherit the kingdom prepared for you. For I was hungry, you gave me food, sick you cared for me, naked you clothed me . . . As long as you did this to other, you did it to me."[17]

Conclusion: A Synthesis.

The Holy Teaching of Vimalakirti and the New Testament share many common views on love and compassion. In the Vimalarkirti, the love and compassion the Buddha is timeless and unlimited, so also is the love and compassion of Jesus. In the Vimalakirti, without love and compassion one cannot achieve liberation. In the New Testament, love and compassion is also the basis for salvation. In addition, the love of the bodhisattva, as contained in the Vimalakirti is tolerant, pure, moral, selfless, patient, and free from grasping.[18] In the New Testament, the Christian love is also patient and kind, never boastful, rude or selfless. It is the basis of morality.[18]

The major difference between the concept of love and compassion in the Vimalakirti is that love in the New Testament presents the notion of self first, 'love your neighbor as your self,'[19] while in the Vimalakirti, there is no-self at all. Again, the New Testament expression of compassion, especially, when Christians express it others, involves some element of pity, while the compassion of the bodhisattva is free of pity.

Notes.

1. Robert A. F. Thurman, *The Holy Teaching of Vimalakirti.* (Pennsylvania: The

Pennsylvania State University Press, 1976), ix

2. The Holy Teaching of Vimalakirti in Pennsylvania State university Website, http://www.psupress.psu.edu/books/titles/0-271-OQ601-3.html (accessed October

4, 2007).

3. Raymond F. Bulman & Frederick J. Parrella, ed., *Religion in the New Millennium: Theology in the Spirit of Paul Tillich.* (Georgia: Mercer University

Press, 2001), 166.

4. The New Testament in Wikipedia the Free Encyclopedia, http://en.wikipedia.org/wiki/New_Testament (accessed October 8, 2007).

5. Thurman, *The Holy Teaching of Vimalakirti*, 43.

6 Ibid., 57.

7. Ibid., 87.

8. Ibid., 22,57.

9. The Srimala Devi Sutra no. 5, http://www.purifymind.com/
SrimalaDeviSutra.htm

(accessed October 4, 2007).

10. Bukkyo Dendo Kyokai, *The Teaching of Buddha.* (Japan:
Kosaido Printing Co.,

1966), 15.

11. Xavier Leon-Dufour, *Dictionary of Biblical Theology.*
(Boston: St. Paul Books,

1995), 323-324.

12. John 3:16.

13. A Word Study on Compassion in the New Testament in
Week of Compassion

Website, http://www.weekofcompassion.org/pages/resources/
Gifts . . . (accessed

Octobe 9, 2007).

14. Matt.9:36; Mtt.l4:14; Mk.6:34; Lk.7:13.

15. Luke 6:36.

16. John 13:34-35.

17. Matt. 25:34-40

18. Thurman, *The Holy Teaching of Vimalakirti.* 57

19. I Cor. 13:4-8

3.6 THE RULES AND RITES OF ORDINATION IN THE BUDDHIST MONASTIC CODE VIS-À-VIS CATHOLIC ORDINATION / PROFESSION IN THE CODE OF CANON LAW.

Introduction.

The rite of ordination in Buddhism and in the Catholic Church makes one a monk, a nun, a priest, and a religious, depending on the religious tradition. Ordination initiates one into the monastic state or priestly state of life. For one to be ordained, there are necessary rules to be followed. What are these rules for the Buddhist monks and nuns, as contained in the Buddhist Monastic Code and what are they for the Catholic priests, monks, and nuns, as contained in the Catholic Code of Canon Law. What are the similarities between these rules in these two different religious traditions? This essay will address these questions.

It will be good to note that monasticism and monastic life is not limited to Buddhism. Many religions of the world do practice it. For us to have a better understanding of the rules of ordination in the Buddhist and Catholic traditions, permit me to give an over view of monasticism in Buddhism and Christianity.

Monasticism in Buddhism and Christianity.

For a proper understanding of the place of ordination in Buddhist and Christian monastic traditions, we have to understand what monasticism is and how it began in these two religious traditions. According to Resse, the term monasticism is, "From the Greek *monazein* ("to be alone"). [It is] a discipline of life characterized by withdrawal from the world, meditation, self-abnegation and degree of asceticism."[1] The members of the monastic family, especially in Buddhism and Catholicism are divided into two: (1) The monks (bhikkhus) who are males, and the "brothers" in the Catholic tradition. (2) The nuns (bhikkhunis) who are females, and the "sisters" in the Catholic traditions. In most traditions like Hinduism and Jainism, the monastic life is limited to men only.

Buddhism: Monastic life in Buddhism is as old as the Buddhist religion, having being founded by the Buddha himself. It is on record that, "The order of Buddhist monks and original nuns was founded by Gautama Buddha during his lifetime over 2500 years ago. The Buddhist monastic life grew out of the lifestyle of earlier sects of wandering ascetics . . . and was initially fairly eremitic in nature."[2] Initially the monks were wandering ascetics. According to the Buddha, "A man who wishes to be my disciple must be willing to give up all direct relations with his family, the social life of the world and all dependence upon wealth. A man who has given up all such relations for the sake of the Dharma and has no abiding place for either his body or mind has become my disciple and is to be called a homeless brother."[3] To become a disciple of the Buddha or a monk, ascetic rules were compulsory. On this, the Buddha taught, "My disciples, the homeless brothers must observe the four rules and build their lives upon them. First, they wear old and cast-off garments; second, they get their food through alms-begging; third, their home is where night finds them as under a tree or on a rock; and, fourth, they use only a special medicine made from urine laid down by the brotherhood."[4] Today, the Buddhist monks and nuns live in the monastery under a community called *Sangha*.

Christianity: When we talk of monastic life in the Christian tradition, we are referring the Catholic Church. Monasticism in Catholicism, though not directly founded by Jesus Christ, is a life modeled after Jesus who abandoned everything and "had no where to lay his head."[5] It is a response to the call of Jesus who said, "If any man comes to me without abandoning his father, mother, wife, and children, brothers, sisters, yes and his own life too, he cannot be my disciple. Anyone who does not carry his own cross and come after me cannot be my disciple."[6]

Monastic life in Christianity began in the 3rd century A.D. In the words of Brooke, "The monastic ideal is commonly reckoned to owe its formation to St. Anthony (c. 251-356), who was the first great anchorite and leader in the Egyptian desert at the turn of the third and fourth century. It is beyond doubt that it was in the deserts of Egypt that monasticism, as a large-scale movement, was born."[7] In the early fifth century Cassian, an Eastern Patriarch, had written what could be called the earliest monastic rule in France. At this time in France and Italy there were monks of a sort though in a confused way.[8] However, it was St. Benedict who laid down the rule of what has survived today as a rule for Christian and Catholic monastic way of life. According to Merton, "The *Rule* of St. Benedict, the "Patriarch of Western Monasticism," is thought to have been composed somewhere around 530 and 540 A.D"[9]

The Catholic monks (brothers) and nun (sisters) live an organized community life in monasteries, nunneries, and convents.

The Rule of Ordination in the Buddhist Monastic Code.

How does one become a Buddhist monk or nun? How is he or she ordained, and what are the rule regarding the ordination? We shall answer these questions here.

The ordination of monks, as we have it today, developed over a period. At the time of the Buddha, for example, it underwent three stages. As recorded in *The Buddhist Monastic Code*, "Like so many other aspects of the *vinaya*, the procedures for ordination – the patterns to be followed in accepting applicants into the community – were not determined at once, but grew in response to events over time. There were three main stages in the development."[10] The first stage was a face-to-face acceptance by the Buddha himself. The second stage involved a delegation by the Buddha of his disciples to accept the applicants using the triple refuge, because of distance and bad road coming to the Buddha. The third stage is, "a formal community transaction, using a motion and three proclamations."[11]

In the *Vinaya* [Monastic Code of Life], the ordination ceremony of a monk is a legal act or transaction of the Sangha. The process is divided into two parts: Going-forth (*pabbajja*) and Acceptance (*upasampada*). We shall discuss these two parts individually for a better understanding.

Going-forth: The Going-forth also referred to as "lower Ordination," though not a community transaction is the first step in the process of ordination. Accordingly,

The ordination procedure for Buddhist monks, known as the 'Going-forth', begins with the applicant's formal request (*pabbajja*) to a senior monk or bhikkhu for the novice (*samanera*) ordination. On receiving permission, the applicant prepares for the ceremony by acquiring a complete set of robes and getting help of the monks in the monastery to shave his head.[12]

According to the Monastic Code, "In the Going-forth, one leaves the home life for the homeless life, becoming a novice. After one's head is shaved, one dons the ochre robes, takes refuge in the Triple Gem [the Buddha, the dharma, and the Sangha], and undertakes the ten precepts."[13] The ordination goes like this:

When handing over the robes to the senior monk, the intended novice say:

Venerable Sir, I respectfully ask you to take this set of robes in my hand and out of compassion ordain me as a novice in order that I may be free from the cycle of existence.

When requesting the robe back from the senior monk, he says:

Venerable Sir, I respectfully ask you to give me the set of robes in my hand and out of compassion ordain me as a novice in order that I may be free from the cycle of existence.

On requesting to be ordained, the novice says:

Venerable Sir, I respectfully ask you to ordain me as a novice in order that I may be free from the cycle of existence and attain Nibbana [Nirvana].

The candidate then takes refuge in the Triple Gem and undertakes the Ten Training Rules or Precepts in Pali. Finally, as a novice, he requests the senior monk to be his preceptor, and being so accepted he receives a new name in Pali.[14]

To qualify for this ordination and for its validity, the Code stipulates that:

An application for ordination must be a male who meets the age requirements, and must not have had any characteristics that would disqualify him from

ordination . . . An applicant for the Going-forth must
be at least fifteen years old or, if not yet fifteen, 'capable
of chasing crows away.[15]

If the above conditions are not met, the ordination is invalid.

Acceptance: This is also called "Higher Ordination." It
constitutes a Sangha or Community transaction. The higher
ordination begins with the inspection of the robes and the
alms-bowl, followed by the given of a new name to the candidate
and his preceptor. The candidate is given the name "Naga", and
his preceptor is named Venerable Tissa. The name, "*Naga*" is in
remembrance of the Snake, *Naga,* who took the human form and
became a monk. As Brahmavamso puts it, "Then out of compassion
for the sad snake, the Lord Buddha said that from then on, all
candidates for the monkhood be called 'Naga' as a consolation.
They are still called 'Naga' to this day."[16] In the Vinaya, the Buddha
decreed that a condition for higher ordination is that the candidate
has a preceptor. Therefore, at the time of novice ordination, the
candidate requests a senior monk to be his preceptor, who upon
acceptance guides the young monk as long as he remains a monk.
Without the higher ordination, one is not yet a bona-fide member
of the Buddhist order of monks. According to the Code, "In the
Acceptance, one becomes a full-fledged bhikkhu, with full rights to
live in common affiliation with the Bhikkhu Sangha."[17]

The given of the new name is followed by an instructions and
questioning. Here are the lists of questions and the applicant to
answers yes or no to them, except for the last two questions that
require him to mention his name and that of his preceptor:

1. Do you suffer from leprosy?
2. Do you have boils?
3. Do you have eczema?
4. Have you tuberculosis?
5. Do you get epilepsy?
6. Are you a human being?
7. Are you a man?
8. Are you a free man?

9. Are you free from government service?

10 Do you have your parents' permission to be ordained?

11. Have you a set of three robes and an alms-bowl?

12. What is your name? (*My name is Naga*)

13. What is your preceptor's name? (*My preceptor's name is Venerable Tissa*).[18]

After the examinations, the ordination proper begins with the senior monk bowing and saying to the assembly:

May the Sangha hear me. The candidate, Naga, under the Venerable Tissa, has been examined. If the Sangha is willing may he be allowed to come forward.

On coming forward, the senior monk addresses him, saying:

Now is the time for you, Naga, to request the Sangha to ordain you a bhikkhu. You request should be both in Pali and in English.

The novice says:

Venerable sir, I respectfully request the Sangha to ordain me a bhikkhu. I beg the Sangha out of compassion to lift me up from the status of a novice. [19] He makes this request three times.

After ascertaining that the novice has no obstacle to his ordination, and no one opposes the ordination through the silence of the Sangha, the senior monk ordains the novice with these words:

The Sangha is silent; therefore, Naga is admitted to the Sangha. Venerable Tissa is his Preceptor. The Sangha is agreed, therefore is silent. I too become silent. [20]

For the ordination to be valid, the Monastic Code or Canon requires two types of validity: validity on the part of the object (the candidate), and validity on the part of the assembly (Sangha). On the part of the object, the Code states,

> An applicant for ordination must be a male who meets the age requirement, and must not have any characteristics that would disqualify him for ordination . . . An applicant for full ordination must be at least twenty years old, counting from the time his consciousness first arose at conception in his mother's womb. [21]

When the age requirement is fulfilled, the candidate must fulfill still other conditions. According to the Code, "A person may be absolutely disqualified if he: 1) has an abnormal gender, 2) has committed any of the five deeds leading to immediate retribution in hell, 3) has seriously wronged the Dharma-Vinaya, 4) if the person is an animal."[22] Other conditions required of the candidate are as follows: He must be without obligation; he must be without serious, disfiguring, or communicable diseases; he must not be a disturber of peace; he must not have been marked with severe punishments; he must not be physically handicapped, feeble, or deformed.[23]

On the part of the assembly, for an ordination to be valid, a quorum must be formed. Regarding what constitute a quorum, the Code stipulates,

> The quorum for full Acceptance in the middle Ganges valley is ten bhikkhus. In the outlying districts (this covers the entire world outside the middle Ganges valley), the quorum is five as long as one of the five is a Vinaya expert.[24]

Another requirement for validity on the part of the assembly is that of the validity of the transaction statement. Without it, the ordination is not valid. According to the Code,

> The transaction statement for full Acceptance consists of a motion and three proclamations. As with all other transaction statements, it should be recited by an experienced, competent bhikkhu. At present, it is often recited by two bhikkhus together. The applicant becomes a bhikkhu when the third proclamation is finished.[25]

In all, Buddhist monks are celibates. Ordination into the Buddhist monastic order is a happy celebration. It is a moment of joy for the Sangha, parents, friends, and the lay people. This is manifested through the various gift offered to the newly ordained monk.

The Rule of Ordination/Profession in the Catholic Code of Canon Law.

In the Catholic Church, there are two ways of initiation into the monastic (religious) state of life and the priestly state of the life. One becomes a monk through the rite of religious profession (not ordination), and one becomes a priest through the rite of ordination. For the sake of clarify, Religious Profession is, "A contract made by taking the public vows in a religious institute when one enters the religious state. It may be perpetual or temporal. It must be made according to the law."[26] Religious profession is not just an ordinary admission into a religious community; it a consecration into a holy state of life. The rite of profession is therefore a consecration of one's life to God. Vatican II teaches that, "By her approval the Church not only raises the religious profession to the dignity of a canonical state. By the liturgical setting of that profession she manifests that it is a state consecration to God."[27]

On the other hand, ordination imprints a sacred character on the person that is ordained. It is for life. According to Broderick, "The term ordination is limited to those rites in which there is a distinct laying on of hands: diaconate, priesthood, and episcopacy – and only those so ordained are considered clerics."[28] A religious (monk) can and may be ordained a priest after some years of profession as a brother or a monk.

The Profession of a Monk: The procedure for becoming a monk begins with admission into the novitiate. When thus admitted, the applicant becomes a novice. The juridic act of admitting to the novitiate belongs to the major superiors according to the proper law of the institute. The proper law can require the advice or consent of the council. In exercising this function, the Code of Canon Law stipulates that,

> Superiors are to be vigilant about admitting only those who, besides the required age, have health, suitable character and sufficient qualities of maturity to embrace the particular life of the institute; this health, character,

and maturity are to be attested to, if necessary by using experts.[29]

As mentioned in the above canon, age and health are necessary requisite for the admission of a novice, in addition to other requirements enunciated in the Code. According to Canon 643, one is invalidly admitted to the novitiate:

1. Who has not yet completed the seventeenth year of age;
2. who is a spouse, during a marriage;
3. who is presently held by a sacred bond with any institute of consecrated life or who is incorporated in any society of apostolic life;
4. who enters the institute as a result of force, grave fear, or fraud, or when the superior receives induced in the same way;
5. who has concealed his or her incorporation in any institute of consecrated life or society of apostolic life.[30]

When one is admitted, he undergoes a period of formation lasting two to four year. Upon the recommendation of the formators and major superior, the novice is professed a monk. In the profession, the monk takes three vows known as the evangelical counsel, which include the vows of chastity, poverty, and obedience.

There are two types of profession: temporary and perpetual profession. According to the Code, "Temporary profession is made for the time defined in proper law, which may not be less than three years and no longer than six years."[31] For the temporary profession to be valid certain rules must be followed and the candidate must fulfill certain conditions. The Code laid down the following rules,

> For the validity of temporal profession, it is required that: 1) the person who is about to make the profession shall have completed at least the eighteenth year of age; 2) the novitiate has been validly completed; 3) admission has been freely given by the competent superior with the vote of the council in accord with the norm of law; 4) the profession be expressed and made without force,

grave fear or fraud; 5) the profession be received by the legitimate personally or through delegation. [32.]

When the duration of temporary profession elapses, the monk may renew his profession or apply for the perpetual profession. If he does not want to renew his vows or apply for final or perpetual profession, he is free to live the order. For the perpetual profession, all the rules apply as in the temporary profession except that the monk or brother must be at least twenty-one years of age at the time of final profession, and must have stayed in the order for at least a period of six years.

The rite of profession goes this may:

A senior monk calls out the one to be professed and he responds saying:

Behold, Lord, you have called me.

The prelate (Bishop) will then question the candidates thus:

Dear son, what do you ask of God and His holy Church?

Candidate: *I ask to be allowed to make solemn profession in our Order for the glory of God and the service of the Church.*[33]

This is followed by the examination of the candidate by the prelate. The candidate will declare his intention and resolve to strive steadfastly for perfection in the love of God and neighbor by living out the Gospel with all his hearts and in keeping the rules of the Order. After the invocation of the saints, the candidate pronounces his vows of religious profession thus:

> I, Brother *N*, offer and give myself to the Church of *N*, and I promise a conversion of my ways and life in community, especially in poverty, consecrated celibacy and obedience, according to the Gospel of Christ and the apostolic way of life, according to the Rule of St. Augustine and the Constitutions of the Order of Premontre; I promise this before N, the prelate of this canonry and before this community. [34]

Having pronounced the vows, the superior of the Order welcomes him as a member of the religious community of monks or brothers. In this community, all forms of private ownership are prohibited. The monks living in a particular monastery share everything. This is clearly expressed in the monastic *Rules of St. Benedict,*

> The vice of private ownership must be uprooted from the monastery. No one, without the abbot's permission, shall dare give, receive or keep anything, nothing at all. Monks have neither free will nor free body, but must receive all they need from the abbot. They must keep nothing unless permitted or given them by the abbot. [35]

Ordination of a Priest: The journey to the Catholic priesthood begins with the spiritual and academic formation from the minor seminary to the major seminary. One is not ordained until he has adequately completed the period of formation, except by a canonical dispensation. As expressed in the *Code of Canon Law,* "Those who aspire to the diaconate or the presbyterate (priesthood) are to receive an accurate formation in accord with the norm of law."[36] The period of formation is to ensure that the candidate cultivates the integral faith, right intention, good morals and proven virtues, good reputation, physical and psychological, and possesses the required knowledge, without which he is not ordained a priest.

There are two stages of ordination: the diaconate and the priestly ordinations. For one to qualify for either the diaconate or the priestly [presbyterate], he must be free of all impediments and irregularities, and must declare his freedom to accept ordination. He must also have completed or reached the minimum age of ordination. According to the Code,

> The presbyterate is not to be conferred upon those who have not yet completed the age of twenty-five and who do not possess sufficient maturity; an interval of at least six months is to be observed between the diaconate and

the presbyterate; men destined for the presbyterate are
to be admitted to the order of diaconate only after have
completed the age of twenty-three. [37]

The rite of ordination is divided into fourteen parts:

◊ The Liturgy of Word;
◊ Calling of the Candidates;
◊ Presentation of the Candidates;
◊ Election by the Bishop and Consent of the People;
◊ Homily;
◊ Examination of the Candidates;
◊ Promise of Obedience;
◊ Invitation to prayer and Invocation of the Saints;
◊ Laying on of Hands; Prayer of Consecration;
◊ Investiture with Stole and Dalmatic/Chasuble (Robes);
◊ Anointing of Hands;
◊ Presentation of Gifts;
◊ Kiss of Peace;
◊ Liturgy of the Eucharist.[38]

The proper of ordination begins with the calling out of the
candidate for ordination by a senior priest, who is ceremoniously
referred to as an Archdeacon:

Archdeacon: *Let him who is to be ordained priest please come
forward.*

When the candidate stands out, the Archdeacon presents him
to Bishop, who is the ordaining prelate, saying:

Archdeacon: *Most Reverend Father, holy mother Church asks you
to ordain this man, our brother, for service as a priest.*

Bishop: *Do you judge them worthy?*

Archdeacon: *After inquiry among the people of Christ and upon
recommendation of those concerned with his training, I testify that he
has been found worthy.*

Bishop: *We rely on the help of the Lord God and our Savior Jesus
Christ, and we choose this man, our brother, for service in the prebyteral
order.*

This action is followed by the homily after which the Bishop examines the candidate thus:

Bishop: *My son, before you proceed to the order of the prebyterate, declare before the people* your intention to undertake the office.

Bishop: *Are you resolved, with the help of the Holy Spirit, to discharge without failure, office of the priesthood in the presbyteral order as a conscientious fellow worker with the bishops in caring for the Lord's flock?*

Candidate: *I Am*

Bishop: *Are you resolved to celebrate the mysteries of Christ faithfully and religiously as the Church has handed them down to us for the glory of God and the sanctification of God's people?*

Candidate: *I Am*

Bishop: *Are you resolved to exercise the ministry of the word worthily and wisely, preaching the Gospel and explaining the Catholic faith?*

Candidate: *I Am*

Bishop: *Are you resolved to consecrate your life to God for the salvation of his people, and to unite yourself more closely to every day to Christ the High Priest, who offered himself for us to the Father as a perfect sacrifice?*

Candidate*: I Am With the Help of God.*[39]

After the prayer of consecration and lying on of hands, and the investiture with priestly garment, the candidate becomes full-fledged Catholic priest.

A Synthesis of Rules of Ordination in the Buddhist Monastic Code and Catholic Code of Canon Law.

The Buddhist Monastic Code and the Catholic Code of Canon Law share many things in common on the rules of profession and ordination. In both Codes, profession and ordination are never private affairs. They are always public affairs involving the whole Sangha and the whole Church in Buddhism and Catholicism, respectively. Both Codes lay down specific rules and prescribe rites to be followed. In other words in Buddhism and Catholicism, ordinations are not done casually or haphazardly; they are carefully thought-out and well planned in terms of process, and celebrated solemnly.

Again, no one is forced to become a monk or priest in both traditions. Those to be ordained must on their own express their freedom and consent to accept ordination. Equally, in both Codes, celibacy is obligatory. The Buddhist monastic code requires that monks remain unmarried for life. The same state of life is stipulated in Catholic Canon for monks and priests.

Although, one is expected to be a monk or a priest for life, both Codes agree that they are cases or offences can send one out of the monastic or priestly state back to a lay life. In the Buddhist Monastic Code, one of such cases is the four defeats (parajika). Any monk who commits any of them goes back to lay life. The defeats are, Sexual acts; Stealing; Deprivation of life (killing), and False claim (presenting false identity).[40] In the Catholic Code, there are six irregularities among other things that automatically laicize a priest. The Code states:

> The following are irregular as regards the reception and exercise of orders: A person who labors under some form of insanity or other psychic defect; a person who has committed the delict of apostasy, heresy or schism; a person who has attempted marriage, even a civil marriage only; a person who has committed voluntary homicide or who has procured effective abortion and all persons who positively cooperated in either; a person who has seriously and maliciously mutilated himself or another person or a person who has attempted suicide; a person who has performed an act of order which has been reserved to those who are in the order of episcopate or presbyterate while the person either lacked that order or had been forbidden its exercise by some declared or inflicted penalty.[41]

Conclusion:

Although there are striking and amazing similarities between the rule of ordination in the Buddhist Code and the Catholic Code, there are still differences. Such are seen in the practice of their faith and exercising the duties of ordained persons. Again, even though both traditions emphasis the importance of age, the minimum age requirements are not the same.

In sum, the differences, not withstanding, the similarities are obvious. Both traditions share many things in common regarding ordination, and in the spirit of interfaith and openness, they can learn from each other.

Notes.

1. William L. Reese, *Dictionary of Philosophy and Religion.* (New York: Humanity Books, 1999), 491.
2. "Monasticism" in Wikipedia, *The Free Encyclopedia.* http://en.wikipedia.org/wiki/Monasticism (accessed October 29, 2007)
3. Bukkyo Dendo Kyokai, *The Teaching of the Buddha.* (Japan: Kosaido Printing Co., Ltd, 1966), 194.
4. Ibid., 195.
5. Matthew 8: 20.
6. Luke 14: 26-27.
7. Christopher Brooke, *The Age of Cloister.* (New Jersey: HiddenSpring, 2003), 28.
8. Thomas Merton, *Pre-Benedictine Monasticism: Introduction into the Monastic Tradition 2.* (Michigan: Cistercian Publication, 2006), 3.
9. Ibid.
10. Thanissaro Bhikkhu, *The Buddhist Monastic Code II.* (U.S.A: Thanissaaro Bhikkhu, 2007), 220.
11. Ibid.
12. "The Buddhist World: Theravada Monks Ordination Procedure" in *Buddhist Studies.* http://www.buddhanet.net/e-learning/buddhistworld/ordination1.htm (accessed October 30, 2007)

13. Thanissaro Bhikkhu, *The Buddhist Monastic Code II*, 221.

14. The Buddhist World, Ibid.

15. Bhikkhu, *The Buddhist Monastic Code II* ,221.

16. Ajahn Brahmavamso, Vinaya: *The Ordination Ceremony of a Monk.* http://www.budsas.org/ebud/ebsut020.htm (accessed October 30, 2007).

17. Bhikkhu, *The Buddhist Monastic Code II.,* 221.

18. The Buddhist World, accessed October 30, 2007.

19. Ibid.

21. Bhikkhu, *The Buddhist Monastic Code II.,* 221.

22. Ibid., 222.

23. Ibid., 227-232.

24. Ibid., 235.

25. Ibid., 238-239.

26. Robert C Broderick*, The Catholic Encyclopedia.* (New York: Thomas Nelson Publishers, 1976), 496.

27. Vatican II: *Lumen Gentium*, 45.

28. Broderick, *The Catholic Encyclopedia*, 439.

29. Code of Canon Law, Canon 642

30. Canon 643.

31. Canon 655.

32. Canon 656.

33. "Liturgical Rites: Profession." http://www.premontre.org/ subpages . . . (accessed November 1, 2007).

34. Ibid.

35. Anthony C. Meisel and M. L. del Mastro, trans. *The Rule of St. Benedict* (New York: Image Books, 1975), 76.

36. Canon 1027.

37. Canon 1031.

38. "Ordination Rite – Order of Priest" in *St. Lawrence Roman Catholic Site.* http://www.carr.org/~meripper/0-priest.htm (accessed November 1, 2007)

39. Ibid.

40. Bhikkhu, *Monastic Code I*, 43-108.

41 Canon 1041.

CHAPTER FOUR

ESSAYS ON ISLAM

4.1 ISLAM: BRIEF HISTORICAL FACTS.

Islam originated in Mecca in the present day Saudi Arabia. It was founded by Muhammad in AD 610 as a result of his encounter with Allah's messenger, Angel Gabriel. Islam is a monotheistic religion, believing in Allah as the one and only God. While it is not the largest religion in the world, it is reputed to be the fastest growing and the second largest religion with an estimated population of 1.6 billion adherents.

Although Islam believes in the Jewish Torah and the Christian Gospel as Scriptures, its major source of doctrines and teachings remains the Holy Quran.

4.2 APPLICATIONS AND MISAPPLICATIONS OF THE CONCEPT OF JIHAD FROM THE POINT OF VIEW OF ISLAMIC ORTHODOXY.

Introduction.

In recent times, especially in the West, Islam has been branded 'a religion of war', 'a religion of violence', and after 9/11, a terrorist religion. Expressing this view, one of the Western authors, Robert Spencer, gave the following descriptions about Islam, "Muhammad: Prophet of War . . . The Qur'an: Book of War . . . Islam: Religion of War . . . Religion of Intolerance."[1] Reflecting on the negative attitude towards Islam, Reza Aslan observed that, "Islam has often been portrayed, even by contemporary scholars, as 'a military religion, [with] fanatical warriors, engaged in spreading their faith and their law by armed might' . . ."[2] One of the reasons for these negative attributes of Islam, which by its etymology is a religion of peace, is the concept of **jihad** as one of the official and basic teachings of Islam. But does jihad mean war, violence, and terrorism? Again, can jihad, when misapplied, lead to war, violence, and terrorism? When and how can Muslims perform the binding religious duty of doing a jihad? These, and perhaps many more questions that may arise in course of this discussion, is what this presentation will address.

Jihad: A Holy War?

Ordinarily, when people hear or come across the word **jihad**, what readily comes to mind is a **Holy War.** But does jihad truly mean a holy war? The answer is No. What then is a jihad? Islamic scholars have different interpretations and applications of the term jihad. According to Hunt Janin and Andre Kahlmeyer:

> One of the reasons that *jihad* can mean different things to different peoples, both Muslims and non-Muslims, is that it appears in divergent and even contradictory Quranic texts. Doctrinally, these texts reflect four successive categories in the evolution of Muhammad's own thought. They echo the growth of Islam from its

early, feeble beginning in Mecca (610-622) to its later dominant position in Medina (622-632). The four categories are:

◊ Those which encourage potential converts, by peaceful persuasion, to become Muslims.

◊ Those which enjoin defensive fighting to ward off aggression.

◊ Those which approve, within certain limits, taking the arms in launching attacks.

◊ Those which urge the faithful to attack at all times and in all places.[3]

One such Quranic passage that leads to misinterpretation and misrepresentation of Islam and jihad is Surah 9: 5, 29. It states,

But when the forbidden months are past, then fight and slay pagans wherever you find them, and seize them, beleaguer them, and lie in wait for them in every stratagem . . . Fight those who do not believe in Allah nor the Last Day, nor hold that forbidden which has been forbidden by Allah and His Messenger, nor acknowledge the Religion of truth, (even if they are) of the People of the Book, until they pay the Jizya with willing submission, and feel themselves subdued.[4]

From the point of view of Islamic orthodoxy, and based on official teachings of Islamic authority, jihad does not mean war or holy war. According to Suzanne Haneef, The Arabic word *jihad* means striving."[5] From the Arabic root of this word, its proper religious meaning is drawn in Islamic orthodoxy. Jihad, therefore,

In its primary religious connotation (sometimes referred to as "the greater jihad"), means the struggle of the soul to overcome the sinful obstacles that keep a person from God . . . However, because Islam considers this inward struggle for holiness and submission to be inseparable from the outward struggle for the welfare of humanity, jihad has more often been associated with its secondary connotation ("the lesser jihad"); that is, any exertion – military or otherwise – against oppression and tyranny.[6]

Expressed in another way, Haneef said,

The greater jihad [is] within the self. Consequently, when we are serious about our religion, we are involved in a life-long struggle between our souls and its enemies: Satan, our *nafs,* its passions, and worldly attractions. Part of this struggle involves fighting against negativity and destructive energies, which are tools of Satan, both within ourselves and in our surroundings."[7]

One thing that should be emphasized is that this striving or struggle is not for selfish purposes. For it to be a jihad, it must be in the cause of Allah. As such, "All everyday struggles in life to please God can be considered jihad. The struggle to build a good Muslim society is a kind of jihad . . . Self-control is also a great jihad. Taking up arms in defense of Islam is also a kind of jihad."[8]

Applications of the Concept of a Jihad.

From the point of view of Islamic orthodoxy, not all actions of striving or struggling or fighting (especially armed struggling or fighting), qualifies to be called a jihad in the name of Islam. There are rules that determine the proper applications of the concept of a jihad. For a war to be called jihad, it must have the authority of a legitimate Islamic leader, and certain rules must be applied. An attack that is occasioned by *fatwa* issued by an individual Muslim is not a jihad and does not get the endorsement of Islamic orthodoxy. According to Janin and Kahlmeyer, "The classical medieval theory of jihad contained elaborate rules for the onset, conduct, interruption and cessation of war, for the use of weapons, and the treatment of prisoners. No war could be considered a jihad unless it was formally authorized and led by the legitimate religious and political authorities. Islam's enemies were to be given fair warning before they were attacked."[9]

Highlighting some of the rules guiding the proper application of a jihad according to Islamic orthodoxy, Aslan said, "Thus, the killing of women, children, monks, rabbi, the elderly, or any other noncombatant was absolutely forbidden under any circumstances. Muslim law eventually expanded on these prohibitions to outlaw the torture of prisoners of war; the mutilation of the dead; rape, molestation, or any kind of sexual violence during combats; the killing of diplomats, the wanton destruction of property, and the demolition of religious or medical institutions . . ."[10] Islam strictly forbids fighting and killing, except in self—defense, especially in matters of faith, oppression and injustice. The Qur'an, 2:190 is quite clear on this, "Fight in the cause of Allah those who fight you, but do not transgress limits; for Allah does not love transgressors." Consequently, "Acts of terrorism or attacks on civilians are strictly prohibited and detestable in Islam, even if they should happen to be done by individuals claiming to be Muslims."[11]

In Islamic orthodoxy, therefore, a proper application of the concept of a jihad begins with an individual Muslim, who must strive daily to overcome his imperfection and submit his will to Allah, and when it becomes extremely necessary to take up arms, it must be done according to the regulations mentioned above; otherwise it is not a jihad in the name of Islam.

Misapplication Of The Concept Of A Jihad.

Although we have seen the strict conditions under which war or fighting in the name of Islam can be called a jihad, in our society today there is evidence of acts of violence, terrorism, and suicide bombing under the umbrella of Islamic jihad. In the eyes of Islamic orthodoxy, these are misapplications of the concept of jihad.

Let us cite few examples of these misapplications. Waging war that is politically and socially motivated, which has no religious basis, under the guise of a jihad is a misapplication. As beautifully expressed by Janin and Kahlmeyer, " . . . not all conflicts that the combatants call *jihad* are fought over matters of principle and belief . . . Muslims often invoke jihad purely as a political and a propaganda weapon . . . The politically motivated clashes between India and Pakistan over Kashmir are another good case in point."[12] Re-echoing the point made by Janin and Kahlmeyer, Aslan noted that " . . . while [the] definition of jihad has occasionally been manipulated by militants and extremists to give religious sanction to what are in actuality social and political agendas, that is not at all how Muhammad understood the term."[13]

In many countries of the world, they have been, and are still going on, many violent and terrorist activities which are branded Islamic jihad, which properly speaking is a misapplication of the concept of a jihad. One clear example is the 9/11 episode.

Describing and placing the attack in its proper context, Aslan said:

> Osama bin Laden, who . . . eventually put into practice his mentor's (Abdullah Yusuf Azzam) ideology by calling for a worldwide Muslim campaign of jihad against the West, thus launching a horrifying wave of terrorism that resulted in the deaths of thousands of innocent people. Of course, these attacks (in Iraq, Afghanistan, America, etc) are not defensive strikes against specific acts of aggression. They are not sanctioned by a qualified *mujtahid*. They make no differentiation between combatant and non combatant. And they indiscriminately kill men, women, children, Muslim and non-Muslim. In other words, they fall short of the regulations imposed by Muhammad for a legitimate *jihadi* response, which is why despite common perception of the West; they are so roundly condemned by vast majority of the world's Muslims, including some of Islam's most militant and anti-American cleric such as Shaykh Fadlallah, the

spiritual leader of Lebanon's Hezbollah, and the radical Muslim televangelist Yusuf al-Qaradawi.[14]

It is evident from the above expositions that there have been terrible misapplications of the concept of jihad in Islam by various Muslim individuals and groups. It is these misapplications that portray Islam as a religion of war and violence.

Conclusion.

It must be pointed out that in almost all of the majority religions of the world, not just Islam, they have been cases where adherents have committed violent actions in the name of their religion without receiving the blessing and approval of their religious authorities. Hence, violence committed by members of a religious body should not be confused with the official and orthodox teaching and doctrinal stand of such religion against acts of terrorism, violence, oppression, and injustice. Just as it wrong to brand Christianity a religion of war because of the crusades, so also it is wrong to brand Islam a religion of violence because of some violent activities wrongfully applied as a jihad by Muslim fundamentalists.

NOTES
1. Robert Spencer, *The politically Incorrect Guide to Islam (and the Crusades).* (Washington D.C: Regnery Publishing, Inc., 2005), xiii.
2. Reza Aslan, *No god But God.* (New York: Random House, Inc., 2006), 78.
3. Hunt Janin and Andre Kahlmeyer, *Islamic Law: The Sharia from Muhammad's Time to the Present.* (Jefferson: McFarland & Company, Inc., 2007), 106.
4. The Holy Qur'an 9:5, 29.
5. Haneef Susanne, *Islam: The Path of God.* (Illinois: Library of Islam, 1996), 128.
6. Aslan, *No god But God*, 81.
7. Haneef, *Islam: The Path of God*, 128.

8. Mark Water, *Encyclopedia of World Religions, Cults, and Occul.* (Tennessee: A. M. G. Publishers, 2006), 121.

9. Janin and Kahlmeyer, *Islamic Law: The Sharia from Muhammad's Time to the Present,* 108.

10. Aslan, *No god But God,* 84.

11. Haneef, *Islam: The Path of God,* 98.

12. Janin and Kahlmeyer, *Islamic Law: The Sharia from Muhammad's Time to the Present,* 107.

13. Aslan, *No god But God,* 81.

14. Ibid, 86-87

4.3 THE IDEA OF PROPHECY IN ISLAM CONTRASTED WITH THE IDEA OF PROPHECY IN ROMAN CATHOLICISM.

Introduction.

One common theme that appears in Christianity and Islam is the belief in prophets and prophecy. Together with Judaism, Christianity and Islam are classified as prophetic religions. In the words of John F. Haught, "They (Judaism, Christianity, and Islam) all have a special relationship to the theme of promise. And because of the prominence in these three traditions of the figure of the "prophet" who proclaims the divine promise, they may be called prophetic religions."[1]

Although Christianity and Islam share a belief in prophecy, their understanding and approach to prophecy and prophetic ministry differ considerably. Even among Christians, the Catholic Church has a different approach and idea of prophecy as distinct from other Protestant churches, especially, the Evangelical, Pentecostal, and New Age churches.

The main focus of this paper is the study of the idea of prophecy found in Islam and Catholicism. How do these religions understand prophecy, how do they differ and how do they relate in their ideas and understanding?

The Prophet and Prophecy.

The word "prophecy" and who a prophet is means different thing to different people and different religions. To some people, the prophet is one who foresees or foretells the future. To such people, therefore, prophecy would mean predicting the future. To some still, the prophet is spokesman, especially of God, or gods. As a spokesman, he is also an intermediary between God and people. To this group of people, prophecy would mean speaking and telling people what God expects or demands of them.

Etymologically, the word prophecy is derived "from the Greek *prophetein* (the gift of interpreting the will of he gods). Interpreting the will of the gods sometimes but by no means always, implied the prediction of future events. In Greek religion, it was applied to those who interpreted dreams, visions, and enigmatic utterances of the oracles."[2]

According to the Catholic Encyclopedia, "A prophecy is a message of truth received from God and transmitted by a prophet who serves as the intermediary between God and the people; it tells of future events that could not otherwise be known."[3] Accordingly, prophecy is not primarily a matter of predicting the future. But insofar as the prophet offers an interpretation of events and discusses the consequences of one form of action or another, or of a failure to act, the prophet is indeed concerned with the future.

Biblically, "The prophet is one who, literally, is called to speak on behalf of another, in this case on behalf of God (Hebrew, *nabi*). The prophet, as opposed to the institutional figure, stands apart from his or her own society, as critic and judge. The prophet proclaims a message which makes demands. Insofar as the prophet claims to speak on behalf of God, the revelation as well as its interpreter . . . The word of God comes to the prophet, not for the prophet's own good, but for the community's."[4] The true prophet in the Christian understanding, therefore, is one who is related to the Word Incarnate of God. He exists as a prophet to bring God's revealed message to men that necessarily is rooted in future. For all of God's communications with man are aimed eventually in a linear progression into the future, leading man into God's eternal life.

Pre-Islamic Arabia was already familiar with prophecy and the role of a prophet in the life of the society and the people. It is on record that, "Pre-Islamic prophecy in Arabia was no different in character from other Semitic prophecy. Pre-Islamic terms for prophet are *'arraf* and *kahin* ("seer," cognate to Hebrew *kohen*, "priest"). The kahin could often be a priest, and as a diviner he was ecstatic. The kahin was considered to be possessed by a *jinni* ("spirit"), by means of whose power miracles could be performed."[5]

The notion of prophecy and the prophetic ministry in Pre-Islamic Arabia was change or rather transformed with the rise of Muhammad, the prophet of Islam. Expressing this transformation of the prophet from being a seer, visionary, diviner, priest, and someone possessed by a spirit to a messenger of God's word in Arabia, Seyyed Nasr explained:

> Prophethood is according to the Islamic view, a state bestowed upon men whom God has chosen because of certain perfections in them by virtue of which they become the instrument through whom God reveals His message to the world. Their inspiration is directly from Heaven. A prophet owes nothing to anyone. He is not a scholar who discerns through books certain truths, nor one who learns from other human beings and in turn transmits this learning. His knowledge marks a direct intervention of the Divine in the human order, an intervention which is not, from the Islamic point of view, an incarnation but a theophany.[6]

Having discussed the various understandings of prophecy and who the prophet is from the perspective of various people and religions, we shall now discuss the notion or idea of prophecy in Islam in particular.

The Islamic Notion of Prophecy.

In Islam, when one thinks of prophet and prophecy what comes to mind immediately is no person other than Muhammad (May God's blessing and peace be upon him), who in Islam is profoundly called 'the Prophet.' According to Seyyed Hossein Nasr, "When in any Islamic language one says *the* Prophet, it means Muhammad . . . It is even legitimate to say that, in general, when one says *the* Prophet it means the prophet of Islam; . . . the prophet is the prototype and perfect embodiment of prophecy and so in a profound sense is *the* Prophet. In fact in Islam every form of revelation is envisaged as a prophecy whose complete and total realization is to be seen in Muhammad – Upon whom be peace."[7]

Basically, Islam believes that God has sent prophets to every nation and culture at one time or the other. These prophets spoke to their people in their native tongues. Allah, recorded in the Holy

Qur'an, revealed to the Prophet Muhammad thus, "To very people was sent a messenger . . . We did not send a messenger except to teach in the language of his own people, in order to make things clear to them."[8] There were thousands of prophets, according to Islamic tradition, throughout various ages, peoples, and nations before the visible manifestation of the Prophet Muhammad. As expressed by Seyyed, there are one hundred and twenty-four thousand prophets whom God sent before Muhammad.[9] It is the general belief in Islam that there is link between all these prophets and Muhammad. The idea of prophecy in Islam is that, "Prophethood is indivisible, and the Qur'an requires recognition of all prophets as such without discrimination. Yet they are not all equal, some of them being particularly outstanding in qualities of steadfastness and patience under trials. Abraham, Noah, Moses, and Jesus were such great prophets."[10]

In Islam all the prophets are categorized into three groups: those who only received the message from God, those who, in addition to receiving the message, have a divine mandate to propagate the message they received, and those who, in addition to the two groups, established new religions based on the message and mandate they received from God. In the words of Seyyed Nasr:

> Although all prophecy implies a meeting of the Divine and human planes, there are degrees of prophecy dependent upon the type of message revealed and the function of the messenger in propagating that message . . . There is first of all the *nabi*, a man who brings news of God's message, a man whom God has chosen to speak to . . . But the message which the receives is not necessarily universal. He may receive a message which is to remain within him and not be divulged openly or is meant to be imparted to only a few in the cadre of an already existing religion . . . There are those belong to another category of prophets, or a new level of prophecy, namely those who not only receive a message from heaven but are also chosen to propagate that message for the

segment of humanity providentially destined for it. The prophet with such a function is called the *rasul*. He is also a *nabi* . . . Above the *rasul* stands the prophet who is to bring a major new religion to the world, the 'possessor of firmness and determination' *(ulu'l-'azm)* . . . There are then all together three grades of prophecy, that of the *nabi,* the *rasul* and the *ulu'l-'azm* . . . The Prophet (Muhammad) was at once a nabi, a rasul and ulu'l-'azm.[11]

Although God has spoken in the past through prophets, in Islam, Muhammad is believed to be the last and the greatest of all the prophets. This Islamic idea of Muhammad as the last and greatest of all the prophets is succinctly captured in the following words:

The particularity of the Prophet which distinguished him from those that came before him is that he is the last of the prophets, the seal of prophecy who, coming at the end of the prophetic cycle, integrates in himself the function of prophecy as such . . . and brought the cycle of prophecy to a close. After him there will be no new *sharia* or Divine Law brought into world until the end of time. There will be no revelation after him, for he marks the termination of the prophetic cycle.[12]

Islam frowns at anyone within the religion who claims to be a prophet or to have relieved a new revelation from Allah, after the Prophet Muhammad. For instance, one of the reasons, among other things that led to Baha'i group breaking away from Islam to becoming an autonomous religion, is their claim and belief that prophecy did not end with the Prophet Muhammad, and that Husayn Ali, who assumed the name *Bahaullah* (the glory of God) is the promised and messiah after Muhammad. In the words of Hopfe and Woodward, Baha'is believe that, "Divine revelation is a continuous and progressive process and that the mission of messengers of God, represent successive stages in the spiritual growth of humanity. Baha'is believed that Bahaullah is the most recent messenger of God, with God's message for humankind today."[13] This is contrary to the idea of prophethood and prophecy in Islam. Little wonder why in Persia the group was 'persecuted' until they completely broke away from Islam.

It is also the traditional belief in Islam that Muhammad pre-existed before all other prophets. This is what is called 'Muhammadan Reality.' This implies that the Prophet Muhammad is not only the last and end of all prophets and prophecies; he is also the beginning of all of them. As expressed by Seyyed:

> Islam considers all prophets as an aspect of the Universal Logos, which in its perspective is identified with the 'Reality of Muhammad,' which was the first of God's creation and through whom God sees all things. As the Muhammadan reality the Prophet came before all the other prophets at the beginning of the prophetic cycle, and it is to this inner aspect of him as the Logos to which reference is made in the *Hadith* 'He [Muhammad] was prophet [the Logos] when Adam was still between water and clay' . . . He thus is inwardly the beginning and outwardly the end of the prophetic cycle which he synthesizes and unifies in his being. Outwardly he is a human being and inwardly the Universal Man, the norm of all spiritual perfection.[14]

This describe the sense in the above quotation, using a Greco-Christian terminology, the Islamic idea of prophecy is the Prophet Muhammad is the *Alpha* and the *Omega* of all prophets and prophecies.

The Notion of Prophecy in Catholicism.

One of the central beliefs in Catholicism is the belief in prophecy and in the prophets. In the Nicene Creed, which Catholics recite every Sunday and on every solemn occasion, it is stated, "We believe in the Holy Spirit . . . He has spoken through the prophets."[15]

The Catholic Church recognizes and reads the Old Testament prophets and prophecies, but she maintains that such prophetic utterances ended with John the Baptist. After John, God no longer speak through prophets but He revealed Himself in and through Jesus Christ, who wraps up in his person all prophecies. As recorded in the Bible, "God has spoken in the past to our ancestors through the prophets, in many ways, although never completely; but in our own time, the last days, he has spoken definitively to us through his son (Jesus)."[16] Jesus Christ is therefore the fulfillment and the accomplishment of the laws and the prophets. The Second Vatican Council (Vatican II), the official magisterium of the Catholic Church, drawing from the revealed word of God, and inspired by the His Spirit affirmed that, "The most intimate truth thus revealed about God and human salvation shines forth for us in Christ, who is himself both the mediator and the sum total of revelation . . . [He] completed and perfected revelation and confirmed it with divine guarantees."[17]

In Catholicism, therefore, Jesus is the eternal prophet. Forever, he remains the Word that existed with the Father, the Word that was incarnated, the Word that was spoken, and the Word that is constantly being proclaimed. In him the message and the messenger are in perfect union. As expressed by George A Maloney, Jesuit Catholic Priest:

> Jesus Christ is *the* Prophet who gives ultimate meaning to all other prophets. If a prophet in the Old and New Testament understanding of *Nabi* is one who stands in the place of God for the rest of his contemporaries, mediating God's word of salvific revelation to mankind, how perfectly must Jesus Christ, the Word of God enfleshed, be the perfect Prophet. Jesus is the unique prophet because in His case the messenger is the message . . . Jesus Christ is the prophet par excellence because He is "inside" the word, effecting and actuating

what the word stands for . . . Above all, He is the Prophet because He gives man an immediate and absolute communication with God that leads eschatologically to man's ultimate salvation. He is the *Alpha*, the beginning of God's unified process of creation, redemption and sanctification. He is also the *Omega*, the goal and complete fulfillment of every human being, created 'according to the Image and Likeness of God' (Gen. 1:26).[18]

Although, the Catholic Church believed that Jesus is the ultimate fulfillment of the entire prophet and the prophecies, she still believes that God constantly gives to his Church the charism or gift of prophecy to proclaim constantly the Lordship of Jesus. That there were prophets in the early Church is attested to by numbers of passages in the Holy Bible. Such passages include Acts of Apostles 11:27; 21:10-11; 13:1-3; 1Corinthians 13:2; 14:3-5, 24-25; Ephesians 2:20; 3:5; 4:11 etc. God continues to be disclosed through events, and signs of time. The essence of this gift to the Church and her members is to continue the work and mission of Jesus Christ. Accordingly, Vatican II states, "Christ the Lord, in whom the entire revelation of the Most High God is summed up, having fulfilled in his own person and promulgated with his own lips the Gospel promised beforehand by the prophets, commanded the apostles to preach it to everyone as the source of all saving truth and moral law, communicating God's gift to them."[19] In this sense, the Catholic Church believes and teaches that all the baptized Christians share in not just the priestly and kingly ministry of Christ, but also in his prophetic office. Expressing this belief, the Catechism of the Catholic Church states that, "The anointing with sacred chrism signifies the gift of the Holy Spirit to the newly baptized, who has become a Christian, that is, one "anointed" by the Holy Spirit, incorporated into Christ who is anointed priest, prophet, and king."[20]

Although, the Church acknowledges the gift of prophecy to her members, such prophetic roles are regarded as private prophecies.

The Church distinguishes between public and private prophecies. All public prophecies ended in and with Jesus, and "no new public revelation is to be expected before the glorious manifestation of our Lord, Jesus Christ."[21] Private prophecies are regarded as a matter of personal opinion of individuals and they are not obligatory for any member of the Catholic Church to accept or to keep. Distinguishing between public and private prophecies Yves DuPont said, "Private revelations (i.e. apparitions and locutions with or without prophecies) are those which have been recorded since days after Christ. Revelations up to the days of Christ are known as public, biblical, or scriptural revelations. Private revelations or prophecies do not belong to the deposit of faith and, as such, not binding upon our faith."[22] Emphasizing more on that, Edward Connor said, "Private prophecy, even if received from God, is not reliable because the prophet is fallible. He can forget, misunderstand or misinterpret. Even when he does not err, those who hear him and transmit the message can err . . . It is largely merely a private opinion."[23]

In sum Catholics believe in prophets and in prophecy, but all public prophecies are consummated in Jesus Christ, the word made flesh, the messenger and the message embodified.

Prophecy in Islam and Catholicism: Convergence and Divergence.

Having explained the idea of prophecy in both religions, we now stand a better chance to outline where they agree and disagree on this very important idea (prophecy).

Prophecy occupies a dominant place in the belief and teachings of both faiths. They both acknowledge the prophet as the bearer of the divine word of God, and not his own word. Both Muslims and Catholics accept the authenticity and authority of the Hebrew prophets (Old Testament).

On the other hand, while Catholics firmly believe that Jesus is the summary and conclusion of all the prophets and prophecies, the Muslims believed that Muhammad, and not Christ is the last of all the prophets.

Again, the Catholic *magisterium* may and do accept private revelation and prophecies, but Islamic law forbids prophets and prophecies, whether public or private, after Muhammad.

Islam acknowledges the prophetic role and status of Jesus, but Catholicism does not accept that of Muhammad. In fact, in the middle ages, some Catholic authorities went to a far extreme of describing Muhammad as the anti-Christ.

Conclusion.

The essence of this research, apart from academic, is to emphasize more our common heritage as Catholic Christians and Muslims who together are part of the Abrahamic faith, rather than those things that divide us. Such is a step towards better appreciation and respect for each other's faith.

Notes.

1. John F. Haught, *What is Religion: An Introduction.* (New York: Paulist Press, 1990), 62.

2. William L. Reese, *Dictionary of Philosophy and Religion.* (New York: Humanity Books, 1999), 611.

3. Robert C. Broderick, *The Catholic Encyclopedia.* (New York: Thomas Nelson Publishers, 1976), 497.

4. Richard P. McBrien, *Catholicism.* (San Francisco: Harper Collins Publishers, 1994), 260-261.

5. *The Centrality of Prophecy in Islam*, in *Britannica online Encyclopedia* http://www.britannica.com/eb/artcle-34071/prophecy (accessed February 7, 2008),

6. Seyyed Hoseein Nasr, *Ideals and Realities of Islam.* (Pakistan: Suhail Academy, 1993), 84.

7. Ibid, 67-68.

8. The Holy Qur'an 10: 47; 14: 4

9. Nasr, *Ideals and Realities of Islam*, 86.

10. *Islam: Prophecy*, in *Britannica online Encyclopedia* http://www.britannica.com/eb/artcle-69145/Islam (accessed February 7, 2008).

11. Nasr, *Ideals and Realities of Islam*, 85-87.

12. Ibid, 84-85.
13. Lewis M. Hopfe and Mark R. Woodward, *Religions of the World, 8th ed.* (New
Jersey: Prentice Hall, 2001), 369.
14. Nasr, *Ideals and Realities of Islam*, 88-89.
15. Broderick, *The Catholic Encyclopedia,* 424.
16. Hebrews 1: 2-3.
17. Vatican II: *Dei Verbum*, nn.2, 4.
18. George A. Maloney, *Listen, Prophets.* (New Jersey: Dimension Books, 1975), 5-6.
19. Vatican II: *Dei Verbum,* no.7.
20. *Catechism of the Catholic Church*, (Rome: Libreria Editrice Vaticana, 1994), 314.
21. Vatican II: *Dei Verbum*, no.4.
22. Yves DuPont, *Catholic prophecy: The Coming Chastisement.* (Illinois: Tan Books and Publishers, 1973), 10.
23. Edward Connor, *Prophecy Today.* (Illinois: Tan Books and Publishers, 1973), i.

CHAPTER FIVE

ESSAYS ON AFRICAN TRADITIONAL RELIGION (ATR)

5.1 AFRICAN TRADITIONAL RELIGION: BRIEF HISTORICAL FACTS.

African Traditional Religion is one the most complex religions in the world, with diverse variations as there are tribes and clans in the African continents. Like Hinduism, it has no one founder and believes and worships multiple gods and deities. It is a polytheistic religion. ATR has no Scripture, its doctrines and teachings are transmitted through oral traditions, folklores, rituals, celebrations, etc.

Considered as an ethnic or tribal religion, ATR is estimated to have a population of about 180,000 adherents.

5.2 ULTIMATE REALITY IN AFRICAN TRADITIONAL RELIGION VIS-À-VIS HINDUISM AND CHRISTIANITY.

Introduction.

The question, "what is the ultimate reality?" has been the thought of many philosophers and theologians. There are diverse views of the Ultimate Reality as they are many philosophical and religious traditions. The Ultimate Reality is generally understood to be that upon which every other existence depends or that towards which everything points or moves to, itself not being a thing. As Kessler puts it, it is source of the class of all things that exits, but not itself a member of that class.[1]

What in African traditional religion is the Ultimate Reality? Since it is said that the Ultimate Reality is not a member of the class of existence, can anything be identified as ultimate in African traditional religion? If there is, is it one or many, transcendent or visible? How does the African concept of the ultimate reality relate to the same concept in other religions especially Christianity and Hinduism? This essay addresses these questions.

The Ultimate Reality in African Traditional Religion.

It appears to be a very simple task to identify what the ultimate reality is in African traditional religion, but in fact, it is not. It has been common for some thinker so identify God as the ultimate reality in African traditional religion. This is a wrong idea or rather very narrow and limited idea. In African traditional religion, there are many things that are not God, which the Africans, in their religious experience owe allegiance to and worship as the ultimate. As Gary Kessler said, "the use of the word God is very tricky and often confusing. By "God", some mean simply that which is ultimate, in which case "God" designates whatever is understood by the term ultimate reality. Others restrict the use of the term to a personal being."[2]

In practical terms, the traditional Africans do not have God but gods. The traditional African does not say, 'God is my witness' but rather 'the gods are my witness.' From studies and from religious experience, the ultimate reality in African traditional religion is properly identified as the DIVINE. This concept of the Divine unites every other thing or all things the African society see as ultimate, owe allegiance to or worship. In the words of Mbiti: "I am using the word 'divine' to cover personifications of God's activities and manifestations, natural phenomena and objects, the so-called 'nature spirits', deified heroes and mythological figures, gods and demigods, 'divinities', 'ancestor spirits' and the likes."[3] The Divine expresses itself in two fundamentally different forms. According to Benjamin C. Ray, "It is generally recognized that there are two fundamentally different forms of Divinity in African traditional religion: the one creator God, who is usually remote from daily religious life, and many lesser gods and spirits, which are constantly involved in every day experience."[4]

Within this concept comes the creator God who is also called the supreme deity, high God, and Supreme Being. It is this Supreme Deity that has been erroneously called the Ultimate Reality in African Traditional Religion by some scholars. It is good to point out here that the one creator God, high God or Supreme God is understood in African religion not in the same sense, as it is understood in Judaism, Christianity and Islam. He is variously and differently understood and represented in each of the African tribes. There is no universality among the tribes regarding his name, function, action and mode of worshipping him. The reason for these differences is that Traditional religions are not universal. They are tribal or national. Each tribal religion is bound and limited among those whom it has evolved. One tribal traditional religion cannot be propagated in another tribal group, as was the case of European Christians propagating their version of Christianity and concept of God to other continents. [5]

There are also the minor deities or gods within the concepts of the Divine. There are thousands of these deities or gods in African traditional religion. They are directly involved in the day-to-day life of the people and claim more of their religious attention, worship and reverence. They inspire more awe than the supreme deity does.

They localized and visualized unlike the supreme deity who is the unseen great god.

Again, within the concept of the Divine also are the spirits. These are ancestral spirits, animistic spirits, and natural spirits seen in various forces of nature. There are millions of them. Put in the words of Hopfe and Woodward:

> Most Africans believe that spirits populates the universe. The earth, the sky and the waters are believed to contain spiritual or life forces. These forces can be beneficial or harmful. In either case, they are subject to prayer, flattery and sacrifice. Because they have direct influence on human life African people try to understand the spirits and seek their favor.[6]

The Ultimate Reality in African Traditional Religion Vis-Avis Christianity and Hinduism.

The ultimate reality, the Divine, in African religion is one and yet expresses itself in many fundamentally distinct ways. That is to say, the Divine is ONE, yet MANY. This one and many is not in the Christian sense of one God, three persons. In Christianity, God who is the ultimate reality is one God in three persons—the TRINITY. In the words of Francis Ripley, "There are three persons in God. God the Father, God the Son, and God the Holy Ghost. These three persons are not three Gods: the Father, the Son, and the Holy Ghost are all one and the same God."[7] The oneness of the Trinity is a unity of essence and a trinity of persons; three persons united as one God. On the other hand, the 'many' in the concept of the Divine is not a subsistence *many.* It is a fundamentally distinct *many.* In other words, the supreme deity or God, the minor deities or gods and the millions of spirits does not subsist in each other as one; they are independent, distinct and autonomous.

They seem to be a closer relationship between the concepts of the Ultimate Reality in African traditional religion and in Hinduism, especially in postclassical Hinduism. As expressed by Hopfe and Woodward:

> Brahman, who is ultimate reality, is at the core of Hindu thought. He (*sic*) is one and undivided. Yet postclassical Hinduism sees him in terms of three forms or functions. Each of these three functions of Brahman is expressed by a god from classical literature: Brahma, Shiva and Vishnu.[8]

Besides being worshipped independently, Hindu gods have wives, who are revered and worshipped as goddesses as well. Devotees may give full religious attention to each of these gods and goddesses by worshipping in their temples, offering sacrifices, prayers, etc.[9] These gods and goddesses are seen as, and worshipped independently in the same way worshipped distinctly and independently in the same way the gods are seen and worshipped in African Traditional Religion. The concept, "Divine," in African Tradition Religion is properly understood in the same way that Brahman is in Hinduism. They are both one and yet many. In the Divine is found the ONE who is the Supreme Being, in it is also the autonomous MANY who are the minor gods, divinities, and spirits.

Conclusion:

As we have seen so far, we can conclude that there is no one deity, all by itself that can be described as the Ultimate Reality in ATR. On the other hand, it can said that it is the "DIVINE" that constitute the Ultimate Reality in African Traditional Religion, and not just the Supreme Being or high god alone, independent of the other deities, divinities and spirit beings.

I wish to point out that although many scholars have discussed African Traditional Religion from the philosophical point of view, there has not been a systematic, philosophical or theological consensus as to what should be universally accepted by all African tribal religious communities to be the nature of the Ultimate Reality. It is my desire that this essay will ignite an intense interest in African scholars and others to research more on the concept of the Ultimate Reality in African Traditional Religion.

Notes

1. Gary, E. Kessler. *Philosophy of Religion: Towards a Global Perspective.*
(California: 1999). P.96.
2. Ibid. P.44.
3. John S. Mbiti. *African Religions and Philosophy.* (Oxford: 1989). P.74.
4. Benjamin C. Ray. *African Religions: Symbols, Rituals and Community, 2nd Ed.*
(New Jersey: 2000). P.25.
5. Mbiti, *African Religions and Philosophy*, P.4.
6. Lewis M. Hopfe & Mark R. Woodward. *Religions of the World, 8th Ed.* (New
Jersey: 2001). P. 52.
7. Canon Francis Ripley. *This is the Faith: A Complete Explanation of the Catholic
Faith, 3rd Ed.* (Illinois: 2002). P. 102.
8. Hopfe & Woodward. *Religions of the World.* P. 92.
9. Ibid, P. 93.

5.3 NINIAN SMART'S SEVEN DIMENSIONS OF RELIGION AS REFLECTED IN AFRICAN TRADITIONAL RELIGION: A COMPARATIVE ANALYSIS.

Introduction.

In his attempt to explain the nature of religion, Ninian Smart raised some vital questions that will always be discussed in the field of religion. He asked, "Is there some essence which is common to all religions? And cannot a person be religious without belonging to any of the religions?"[1] In answering the above-posited questions, he concluded that rather than delving into what religion was in general, it was better to know religion in a particular sense, (e.g. Hinduism, Buddhism, Christianity, Islam, etc). This approach thus led him to propose the principle of the dimensions of religion as a veritable tool to understand the nature of religion and perhaps the meaning of religion, too.

In his work, *The Nature of Religion,* various religions, except African traditional religion, were used to cite examples. Does it mean that African traditional religion is not considered religion or that the dimensions of religion are lacking in it?

In this paper, it is my aim to carefully examine African traditional religion and determine whether the dimensions of religion enunciated by Smart are true of it. If it were true, how would they be seen in the light of Smart's work? How would these dimensions touch or relate to the African person in his or her religious life and experience?

An Overview of Ninian Smart's Dimensions of Religion:

Let me quickly take an overview of the dimensions of religion as enunciated by Smart. This overview is necessary to understand how they are seen in African traditional religion in that one need to know first what these dimensions are and how they are presented and elucidated by Smart.

Looking at the individual religions of the world and their internal pluralisms, Smart thought that there could still be some observable patterns common to them all. These observable patterns were what he called the dimensions of religion. In his own words, "Despite all this, it is possible to make sense of the variety and to discern some pattern in the luxurious vegetation of the world's religions and sub traditions. One approach is to look at the different aspects or dimensions of religion."[2] He identified seven dimensions of religion that are noticeable not only in what are popularly called religion but also in those that are not, namely; Nationalism and Marxism. These 7 dimensions are:

i) The Practical and Ritual dimension.
ii) The Experiential and Emotional dimension.
iii) The Narrative or Mythic dimension.
iv) The Doctrinal and Philosophical dimension.
v) The Ethical and Legal dimension.
vi) The Social and Institutional dimension.
vii) The Material dimension.[3]

i. The Practical And Ritual Dimension: This refers to the laid down practices and rituals which people of every religion follow, (e.g. regular worship, preaching, prayer) and so on. These are common in faiths of a strong sacramental kind, seen in their services, called liturgy. Such is the case in the Eastern Orthodox, and Judaism before 70 A.D, and the Brahmin form of Hinduism. Also, the yoga in Buddhist and Hindu traditions, as well as the silence and meditation in the Eastern Orthodox, fall within this dimension.

ii. The Experiential and Emotional Dimension: This dimension deals with the experience and emotions of the people in the formation and development of religion.

The visions of Muhammad, the conversion of Paul and the enlightenment of the Buddha come to mind here. Experience and emotion is the vehicle through which other dimensions of religion are expressed. Using the words of Smart, "It is obvious that emotions and experiences of men are the food on which the other dimensions of religion feed: ritual without feeling is cold, doctrine without awe or compassion is dry, and myth which do not move hearers are feeble."[4] He also emphasized the role of music in expressing emotion.

iii. The Narrative and Mythic Dimension: This is the story side of religion, and is typical of all religions. These stories, also called myths, do revolve around religious founders, God or gods, saints, heroes, origin of things, edifying stories, apocalyptic stories etc. They may or may not be historical. These stories are at times expressed in ritual celebrations within a particular religion, an example of which is the mass or communion service in the Christian liturgy celebrating the story of the last supper.

iv. The Doctrinal and Philosophical Dimension: In religion, stories are formed into basis of belief called doctrine. For instance, the doctrine of the divinity of Jesus has a connection with the story of his life and the ritual of the mass or the communion service. This dimension forms the intellectual aspect of religion.

v. The Ethical and Legal Dimension: This dimension refers to the laws that a religious tradition or sub tradition incorporates into its fabric. It sets out the moral principles and ethical code, determines the behavioral pattern of the adherents not only in their religious life, but also in their social and political life (e.g. the Islamic *shari 'a* or law).

vi.) The Social And Institutional Dimension: This dimension implies the incarnation and organization of religion in a particular society. Every religious movement is embodied in a group of people, and is formally organized or institutionalized as a church, u*mma,* or *sangha.* There are a variety of relations between organized religions and society at large, such as the Vatican City State and the Church of England. The social dimension also includes the mass of persons attracted to it, and the outstanding individuals who are rallying points within the society.

vii. The Material Dimension: The social and institutional dimension becomes incarnate in material forms such as buildings, works of art, and other creations.

Under this dimension are other material expressions of religion such as sacred places and symbols. The material dimension is meant to move and help believers in their approach to the divine.

Smart's Dimensions of Religion As Seen In African Traditional Religion (ATR).

Having surveyed through the dimensions of religion, I will now examine and see how they are applied to or are seen in African traditional religion (ATR).

i. **The Practical And Ritual Dimension in ATR:** According to Smart, "Every tradition has some practices to which it adheres—for instance regular worship, preaching and prayer."[5] As this is true of every religion used by Smart in citing examples, so it is of ATR. Affirming the stand of Smart on the ritual dimension, and applying it to ATR, I will borrow the words of Hopfe when he wrote, "Every religion has its rituals. These rituals may be simple or complex, or so brief that the laity may perform them several times a day, every day. Mealtime prayers or libations to African ancestors are examples of these simpler rites."[6] Not classified as a 'religion of the book', ATR is more practical and ritualistic than any other religion. Ritual in ATR covers a wide range of African sacred practices, from circumcision to sacrifice, divination to healing, private prayer to public festivals. They are often times, cyclic. According to E. C. Eze,

> Rituals often occur according to the life cycle of the year. There are hunting rituals as well as those marking the rhythm of agriculture and human life. Every deity has its own ritual, including choice of objects for sacrifice, time of day, week, month, or year to make required sacrifices. 7

In ATR, all rituals are directed to the gods either to appease them, to ask for favor, for atonement, for personal healing, or for the good of the society. On this, B. C. Ray said, "Rituals are performed for a variety of purposes: to cure illness, to initiate the young, to diagnose problems, and restore social harmony. They have important social and psychological consequences. They express moral values, reinforce social unity, and provide psychological therapy."[8] Smart's practical and ritual dimension is clearly seen in ATR.

ii. **The Experienntial and Emotional Dimension in ATR:** The experiential and emotional dimension is also dominant in ATR. The

Africans are used to recalling the experiences of their forefathers and ancestors in their religious setting. ATR is also full of numinous experience, because everything is seen as sacred; the gods are seen to be everywhere and are approached with fear and reverence. In Africa, religion is highly emotional. There is no celebration devoid of it. This emotion may be joyful or mournful. The Africans express their religious emotions mainly by singing and dancing. Highlighting the aspect of music in this dimension, Smart said, "One of the main reasons why music is so potent in religion is that it has mysterious powers to express and engender emotions."[9] Traditional African Religion does not seek to combine sounds in a manner pleasing to the ear, but rather to evoke emotions, to communicate and to pass information to worshippers and dancers.

The shamantic type of experience mentioned by Smart is also typical of ATR. As expressed by Eze, "Some spirits and some deities are believed to 'mount' some of the priests during special rituals. The possessed goes into a trance-like state, sometimes accompanied by speaking in 'tongue'. Possession is usually induced by drumming and dancing."[10] This is an intense spiritual experience that carries strong emotions.

iii. The Narrative or Mythic Dimension in ATR: As rightly observed by Smart, "It is typical of all faith (including ATR) to hand down vital stories: some historical, some about mysterious primordial time when the world was in timeless dawn. These stories are called myths."[11] ATR, not considered 'a religion of the books', uses only narratives and myths in passing on religious ideas, beliefs and practices from one generation to another. In the words of E. Eze, "Myths in ATR are popular method of education: they communicate religious knowledge and morality while amusing or frightening those who hear or read them."[12] Most traditional African groups, including the traditional Yoruba of Nigeria and the Dogon of Mali, have intriguing sacred stories or myths that tell how the world, human beings and the important institutions came to be. Such sacred stories generally also underscore the involvement of ancestors and mythical beings in the life and affairs of the community of the physically living. Myth and proverbs go hand in hand in ATR. Rituals and stories are also bound together in ATR, and are celebrated or acted out in the form of festivals and dances. By acting out the myth, they identify with the divine characters and their actions. According to Hopfe and Woodward, "One of the most common characteristics of all religions, basic and advance, is mythology . . . religious rituals re-enact mythology."[13]

In African society, which is also a religious society, "the history of a people is determined by its mythology. Myth takes hold of the pure creative potencies of the members of the social group, giving them shape."[14]

In ATR, it can be said that the mythic dimension is the most important and the most central upon which other dimensions depend for their expressions and authenticity. For example, it is myth that explains the significance of ritual actions and it explains the religious experiences of the ancestors. It is in myth and stories that religious doctrine are transmitted for it explains how and why ethical norms came to be. It tells how society evolved, and it identifies and tells why a place is more sacred as a place of worship.

iv. The Doctrinal and Philosophical Dimension in ATR: African traditional religion does not have scripture or set of written laws. Nevertheless, we still find Smart's doctrinal and philosophical dimension in ATR. According to Mbiti, in his book, *African Religion and Philosophy:*

> Philosophy of one kind or another is behind the thinking and acting of every people, and a study of traditional religions brings us into those areas of African life where, through word and action, we may be able to discern the philosophy behind . . . African philosophical systems are expressed in religion, proverbs, oral tradition, ethics and morals of the society concerned.[15]

To reiterate what Mbiti said, Ejizu explained, "Traditional Africans rely on repetitive speech-form such as myth, proverbs, wise sayings and songs, as well as art-form like sculptures, dance, ritual objects etc, to preserve and impress their key beliefs, ideas, values in the minds of successive generations."[16] Religious doctrines encapsulate and express for the traditional African groups vital information relating to their different areas of awareness: intuitive, physical, aesthetic and social.

v. The Ethical and Legal Dimension in ATR: Every social group evolves its distinct ethical code, has its norms of acceptable behavior, taboos and prohibitions. In Africa, religion is central in formulating and inculcating the promotion and realization of harmonious inter-relationship among individuals and the community. In most cases, it is within the context of initiation rite that some of these ethical norms are explained to the young ones. Extract of this ethical instruction may read like this:

> Now you are big. Never be rude to anyone older than yourself, especially, not your father, mother . . . if you do this your mother and father will die, and you will be poor . . . and no one will care for you. This is a very evil thing. You are big now! Do not do these things to us, Laguru, they are taboos. Never lie (have sex) with young girls. If you do, you will die.[17]

For traditional Africans, there is no dichotomy between religion and morality. Religion plays a crucial role in the ethical dynamics of the different groups. According to Ejizu,

> In the traditional African background, the 'gods serve as police men'. Traditional Africans believe that spiritual beings, especially ancestral spirits guarantee and legitimate the ethical code. Igbo traditional elders demonstrate this by striking their lineage ritual symbol, OFO, on the ground to mark their promulgation of a law or a taboo. They invoke a divine sanction on anyone who will try to oppose or disobey them.[18]

There are taboos and rituals to protect the divine gift of life. Willful murder is an abomination. Abortion is also regarded as an abomination with severe consequences and penalties.

vi. The Social and Institutional Dimension in ATR: In African traditional society, religion enfolds the whole of life. There is no dichotomy between the sacred and the profane. A completely secular world does not exist. Everybody is religious and everything is done religiously. As one of the pioneer colonial officials, who lived and worked among the traditional Igbo of Nigeria from 895-1905, witnessed,

> They (the Igbos) are in the strict and natural sense of the word, a truly and deeply religious people, of whom it can be said, as it has been said of the Hindus, that 'they eat religiously, drink religiously, bathe religiously, dress religiously, and sin religiously'. In a few words, the religion of these natives, as I have endeavored to point out is their existence, and their existence is their religion. [19]

Traditional African peoples also possess important sacred institutions with significant religious dimension that equally further the community ideal. They include sacred kingship institution, sacred groves, divination and masquerades. Each of them generally implies important religious beliefs, supernatural power and authority, and serves as a vital channel for inculcating and promoting the ideal of harmonious living in society by the people. In most cases, the kings are regarded as descendants or incarnations of divine beings, a mythical ancestor, or divinity. Such is the *OOni* of Ife among the Yoruba, the *Asantehene* of the Ashanti Kingdom and the Queen of the Lovedu in South Africa.

vii. The Material Dimension in ATR: In ATR, there is the incarnation of the social dimension and of religion in general into the society. The invisible beings are represented by different kinds of symbols like carved objects, public shrines, sacred altars, and masquerades.[20] Outstanding mountains and hills are also regarded as sacred places for worship in ATR.[21] Certain villages like Nri, Ile-Ife, Dahomy, Igbo-Ukwu, are regarded as important centers of religious life.

CONCLUSION.

The analysis of Smart's dimensions of religion reveals that, it is apparent that those same dimensions of religion seen in the organized, developed, and scriptural religions of the world, are also manifested and abundant in ATR, which, to some scholars, still regard ATR as 'primitive religion'. ATR in a way may be compared to be an 'uncultivated' or at least not fully 'cultivated land' in terms of academic research, as has been the case in other religions that originated in India, China, and the Middle East. It intended that this essay would bring about some input in 'cultivating' the rich field of ATR.

Notes

1. Gary E. Kessler, *Philosophy of Religion: Towards a Global Perspective.*
(California: 1999). 3.
2. Ibid. 4.
3. N/B: The brief survey of Smart's dimensions of religion is gleaned from Gary E.
Kessler, Ibid. PP. 4-8.
4. Ibid. 4.
5. Ibid. 4.
6. Lewis M. Hopfe & Mark R. Woodward, *Religions of the World. 8th* ed. (New
Jersey: 2001). 6.
7. Eze, E. C., "Religion and Philosophy" in *World Era Encyclopedia,* vol. 10. Ed by
Pierre-Damien Mvuyekure (New York: 2003). 274.
8. Gary E. Kessler, *Religions of the World: Towards a Global Perspective.*
(California: 1999). 3.
9. Ibid. 4.

10. N/B: The brief survey of Smart's dimensions of religion is gleaned from Gary E.

Kessler, Ibid. PP. 4-8.

11. Ibid. 4.

12. Ibid, P. 4

13. Lewis M. Hopfe & Mark R. Woodward, *Religions of the World. 8ᵗʰ ed.* (New

Jersey: 2001). P.6.

14. Eze, *Religion and Philosophy*. P. 277.

15. Benjamin C. Ray, *African Religion: Symbols, Rituals, and Community,* 2ⁿᵈ ed.

(New Jersey: 2002). P. 48-49.

16. Kessler, *Religions of the World.* 5.

17. Eze, *Religion and Philosophy*, 300.

18. Kessler, *Religions of the World*, 5.

19. Eze, *Religion and Philosophy*, 284.

20. Hopfe & Woodward, *Religions of the World*, 25-26.

21. William L. Resse, *Dictionary of Philosophy and Religion.* (New York: 1999),

503

22. Mbiti, J. S., *African Religions and Philosophy.* (Oxford: 1989), 2.

23. Christopher Ejizu, *OFO: Igbo Ritual Symbol.* (Enugu:1986), 59.

24. Ikenga-Metu, E., *Comparative Studies of African Traditional Religion,* (Onitsha:

1987), 207.

25. Ejizu, *Religion and Philosophy*, 90.

26. Leonard, A. G., *The Lower Nigeria and Its Tribe.* (London: 1968 ed), 409.

27. Ejizu, *Religion and Philosophy*, 37.

28. Mbiti, *African Religions and Philosophy*, 55.

5.4 THE PLACE OF WOMEN IN SOUTH ASIAN BUDDHISM VIS-À-VIS AFRICAN TRADITIONAL RELIGION.

Introduction

For centuries, the male dominance over women was generally and globally taken for granted. In most cultures, women themselves seem to have internalized and accepted this image of female inferiority as a norm. In most religions of the world, the situation is no less different. Women are either placed at the background or do not play active role in worship and religion.

The essence of this essay is to understand the place of women in South Asian Buddhism and in African Traditional Religion. To properly discuss this topic, we shall limit ourselves to Theravada Buddhism in India, and to African Traditional Religion as practiced in Nigeria. However, we might be drawing some examples outside these limits to illustrate our points.

The Image of Women in Traditional Indian Society

To get a clear picture of women in South Asian Buddhism, we shall look into the place and position of women in the society that gave birth to Buddhism, i.e., the primitive Indian society.

The Indian society that the Buddha lived can be described as a patriarchal society, one that understood the women's role in society in relation to and dependency upon men. In describing the time and place of women, Karen Andrews said, "The historical Buddha lived in northern India at approximately 500 BCE. Women held an extremely subordinate place in the society in which he lived. They spent their lives serving."[1] Affirming what Andrews said, Swarna de Silva noted that the Indian society accorded women an inferior position. Such position accorded to women in the pre-Buddhist Indian society is seen in this brief description of women as contained in the Laws of Manu,

A girl, or a woman, or even an aged one, must do nothing independently of a man, even in her own house. In childhood, a female must be subject to her father, in youth to her husband, when her lord is dead to her son; a woman must never be independent. (Laws of Manu, V, 147-8).[2]

In the traditional Indian society, whose religion was Brahmanism, women were excluded from taking active part and were deprived of prominent roles in religion. The situation would however, not remain the same with the emergence of Buddhism in India.

The Image and the Place of Women in South Asian Buddhism.
The message and the teachings of the Buddha was a big paradigm shift in the traditional society of India with regard to women. The Buddha did teach that women were not second class citizens. Consequently, they could achieve spiritual liberation and enlightenment along the same path like men. This new message of freedom and liberation attracted many women to Buddhism at its infancy, and consequently led to the establishment of the Bhikkhuni (female monastic) order by the Buddha himself.

Although the Buddha affirmed the spiritual equality of men and women in Buddhism, there were indications, as reflected in various sutras, that the Buddha was still influenced by the social inequality accorded to women as inferior or subordinate to men. This is evident in his initial refusal to admit women into his order, and the eventual giving of the eight rules that placed the nuns permanently under the monks. There are also texts in various sutras that attribute to the Buddha as seeing women as evil that must be avoided for spiritual growth. In such texts the stand of the Buddha on the spiritual equality of men and women faced a big question mark. In the *Tale of King Udayana of Vatsa*, the Buddha said,

> Your majesty, you should know that when men have relationships with women, they have close relationship with evil ways. Women can ruin the precepts of purity; they can ignore honor and virtue. They can cause one to go to hell and they can prevent rebirth in heaven. Why should the wise delight in them? The dead snake and

dog are detestable, but women are even more detestable than they are.[3]

In a similar vein, the Buddha is said to have responded thus to Ananda's question on how the monks should relate to women, "As not seeing them, Ananda. But, if we should see them, what are we to do? No talking, Ananda. But, if they should talk to us, Lord, what are we to do? Keep wide awake, Ananda."[4]

Such statements and positions regarding women that were attributed to the Buddha heavily influenced the place of women in South Asia Buddhism, particularly in the Theravada countries of India, where the women's order is extinct, and in Sri Lanka, where the order of nuns is only recently being resuscitated.

Exploring the place of women in Theravada Buddhism of South Asia, Donald Swearer, citing Alan Spongberg, said:

> In Buddhist texts authored by male monastics, women are depicted in various guises: female renunciants attain arahantship and renowned lay women give generously to the sangha, yet women are also seen as threatening to the stability of the male renunciant order and are often depicted as greedy, weak in wisdom, and inferior to men . . . Exploring a wide range of classical Indian Buddhist texts, Alan Sponberg distills four diverse attitudes toward women. He characterizes these attitudes as soteriological inclusiveness, institutional androcentrism, ascetic misogyny, and soteriological androgyny . . . Although Sponberg's analysis attempts only a broad thematic overview, his schema suggests the complexity of the place of women in the Buddhist worldview and the cultural society it reflects.[5]

It can be affirmed from the above quotation that although women are able to pursue the same spiritual quest as men, and become arahants too, historically and religiously they remain subordinate to men, their social importance and economic stability to the society and the monastic order not withstanding. Even in the path of spiritual quest, there are still indications of women's inferiority to men. In the South Asian Theravadin tradition, women can attain enlightenment, and become arahants, but it ends there. They can never reach "the ultimate spiritual attainment, namely, the Buddhahood itself"[6] which is the exclusive prerogative of men, unlike in Mahayanist tradition where a woman cannot only become a bodhisattva but can also reach the Buddhahood.

The Image and the Place of Women in African Traditional Religion.

Africa, like the traditional Indian society, is a patriarchal society. Socially and culturally, women are subordinate, but not inferior to men. Religiously, however, women and men occupy equal place of importance as far as worship, rituals and sacrifices are concerned. There are religious ceremonies that only women can perform, and some that only men can perform. This is not because of women being superior or inferior, but most often because of the nature, demands, and the sex of the deity or deities concerned. As beautifully expressed by J. O. Awolanu:

> Apart from the belief in the Supreme Being, Africans do recognize lesser categories of spiritual forces. These are considered more responsive to the needs of human beings in their secular and religious lives. Theses divinities were created by God to fulfill specific functions. In the cult of these divinities, there are both priests and priestesses who serve at their shrines or temples. However, the sex of the minister is not an indication of the sex of the divinity. Each sex can operate as the messenger of the deity. African traditional religion is therefore less sexiest in its image of the spiritual world as compared to other world religions. It is this factor which has made it possible for both men and women to perform their sacred functions in the worship of God and his functionaries, the divinities, who incidentally are in both sexes.[7]

Religiously, women are seen as sacred, mysterious and powerful. As a result of this, most strong and influential deities in African Traditional Religion bear the feminine image. For example, the Akan of Ghana and the Igbo of Nigeria regard the next deity after the Supreme Being, the EARTH DEITY, as a goddess. Also, in Yoruba land of Nigeria powerful deities such as Oya, Shango, Orisha Oko, Osun and Olosa, are all feminine deities.[8]

Another area of active and equal involvement of women in African Traditional Religion is the area of ritual specialists. Women, like men, share in the office of priesthood, traditional doctors, mediums and diviners. Articulating this view, Kenneth Kojo Anti said:

> In the area of ritual services, women are never left behind or relegated to a subordinate position. For example, the priesthood, which is a highly respected office in African societies, is open to both men and women. They are formally trained and commissioned or called by directly by the deity . . . Women like men are also traditional doctors, healers, or herbalist. Every village in Africa has a medicine-man or woman with reach . . . In general women practice as medium and diviners. Through them spiritual beings make their wishes known to human beings. They relay messages from the other world and also reveal the secrets of the past, present and the future when they are possessed by their deities.[9]

One of the areas that the place of women in African Traditional Religion is so dominant is perhaps in the area of music and dance. African religion is a singing and dancing religion. There are music and dance for every religious event and activity, be it birth, rite of passage, appeasing the gods, communal worship of favor, and thanksgiving before and after harvest, death, funerals etc. In most of these religious activities, the men do the drumming while the women do the singing and the dancing. In most cases, the affairs are completely those of women. Again, to cite Kenneth Anti, "A lot of festivals abound in African Traditional Religions. A good number of them are in honor of the most important divinities and ancestors. Of relevance to us is the phenomenon of singing and dancing by well-dressed women during the celebrations of these festivals . . . with their ritual dances and singing women warm the hearts of the gods."[10] They not only warm the hearts of the gods but they also warm the hearts of the living and add luster to the celebrations.

Although African Traditional Religion promotes the equality and active participants of women in religious activities, there are still apparent prejudices shown to women in African religion by virtue of their sex. According to Anti:

> Though they [women] are regarded as producers of life, they are also seen as spiritual sources of danger. The ritually 'dangerous' nature of women is expressed in notions about the polluting nature of blood, especially the blood of menstruation and of childbirth. It is such notions of pollution which underlie rituals intended to separate 'unclean' women from contact with others . . . Thus in connection with religious functions menstruating women are banned from shrines, neither are they allowed to handle or touch religious objects or personalities.[11]

The above quotation illustrates the reason why virgins and women who have reached menopause are preferred over those who have reached the age of puberty and childbearing, in regard to some sacred duties.

Another area of men's superiority over women in matters of religion is in the attainment of the status of an ANCESTOR. In African Traditional Religion, becoming an ancestor is the ultimate spiritual goal, and "no one can attain ancestral status without having led a morally good life, according to traditional African moral standards. For an ancestor is regarded is regarded as a model or exemplar of conduct in the community, and as source of tribal tradition and of stability."[12] This prestigious status is only attained by men. No matter how morally sound a woman may have lived, even if she were the priestess of the most powerful and influential deity, in African Traditional Religion, especially among the Igbos of Nigeria, she could not and would never become an ancestor.

Evaluation and Conclusion.

So far in this essay, we have analyzed the image and the place of women in South Asian Buddhism and African Traditional Religion. As we have seen, both societies are patriarchal and the image and place of women in religion, to a large extent, are influenced by the societal image of women. One such area is the attainment of the Buddhahood in South Asian Theravadin tradition. Here women could become arahants, but could not and would never attain the status of the Buddha unless they were reborn as men. Similarly, in African Traditional Religion, especially, among the Igbos and Yorubas of Nigeria, women who led good moral lives could become good spirits but they could never become ancestors. Libations are never poured out to them.

However, in placing the role of women in both religions under consideration side by side, I wish to conclude this paper by saying that women occupy a more prominent position of equality with men as priestesses, traditional religious doctors, medium and diviners, sacred and ritual dancers in African Traditional Religion than in South Asian Buddhism.

Notes.
1. Karen Andrews, "Women in Theravada Buddhism." http://www.enabling.org/ia/vipassana/Archive/A/Andrews/womenTheraBud/Andrews.html (accessed February 14, 2008).
2. Swarna de Silva, "The Place of Women in Buddhism." http://www.enabling.org/ia/vipassana/Archive/D/DeSilva/WomeninBuddhism/womenInBud . . . (accessed February 14, 2008).

3. Diana Y. Paul, *Women in Buddhism: Images of the Feminine in Mahayana Tradition.* (Los Angeles: Univ. of California Press, 1985) 30-44.
4. Karma Lekshe Tsomo, ed. *Buddhist Women Across Cultures.* (New York: State Univ. of New York Press, 1999), 51.
5. Donald K. Swearer, *The Buddhist World of Southeast Asia.* (New York: State Univ. of New York Press, 1995), 152.
6. Paul, *Women in Buddhism,* 166.
7. J. O. Awolanu, "Women from the perspective of Religion" in ORITA: *Ibadan Journal of Religious Studies* x/2 Dec. 1976, 99.
8. Jacob K. Olupona, ed. *African Traditional Religion in Contemporary Society.* (New York: Paragon House, 1999), 75.
9. Kenneth Kojo Anti, "Women in African Traditional Religion," http://www.mamiwata.com/women.html (accessed February 16, 2008).
10. Ibid.
11. Ibid.
12. E. Bolaji Idowu, *African Traditional Religion: A Definition.* (New York: Orbis Books, 1975), 179.

CHAPTER SIX

ESSAYS ON MYTHOLOGY

6.1 THE RELIGIOUS ESSENCE OF MYTH.

Introduction

In our civilized world of the 21st Century, one would have thought or assumed that mythical themes and mythologies would no longer exist or appeal to human consciousness. But such assumption has been proved false. Mythical themes, stories and narratives have continued to strive even in an era of historicity, science and technology. More importantly, such themes and stories, directly or indirectly, consciously or unconsciously, keep attracting the attention of elites and mature minds. Contemplating on the ever abiding presence of myth in the contemporary society, Max Muller said, " . . . and yet, how strange are these tales! From the very childhood of philosophy, from the first faintly whispered *why*, to our own time of matured thought and fearless inquiry, mythology has been the ever-recurrent subject of anxious wonder and careful study."[1]

To understand why myth and mythology 'has been the ever-recurrent subject of anxious wonder and careful study,' as Muller noted, even in today's society, one must unavoidably turn to religion. The purpose of this paper is to discuss what myth is, and the role or significance of myth in the formation and development of religion, as well as in the aspects of religious belief, practice, and faith of adherents.

What Is Myth?

The word myth and what it stands for has been variously defined and interpreted by scholars within various text and context without any consensus. Etymologically, the word myth is derived, "From the Greek term *mythos,* meaning, 'legend.' Hence, myth is a narrative account taken to be true, but not known to be true."[2] The word *mythos* has other connotations outside legend. It also stands for stories, sayings, and tales that encompass everything we can possibly think of, ranging from the sacred down to the profane, from the ordinary to the mysterious, and from the physical to the spiritual.

Drawing from the above understanding of myth, Lauri Honko articulated twelve ways by which myth may be described or understood, namely: myth as source of cognitive categories, myth as form of symbolic expression, myth as projection of the subconscious, myth as an integrating factor in man's adaptation to life, myth as character of behavior, myth as legitimation of social institutions, myth as mirror of culture, social and structure, myth as result of historical situation, myth as religious communication, myth as religious genre, and myth as medium for structure.[3]

Generally, myth has been defined simply as story or narrative or even fiction. But it goes beyond a mere story. In the words of Malinowski:

> Myth as it exists in a salvage community, that is in its living primitive form, is not merely a story told but a reality lived. It is not of the nature of fiction, such as we read to-day in a novel, but it is a living reality believed to have once happened in primeval times, and continuing ever since to influence the world and human destinies. This myth is to the savage what, to a fully believing Christian, is the Biblical story of Creation, of the Fall, of Redemption by Christ's sacrifice on the Cross.[4]

Following the same line of thought as Malinowski's, Navone, said, "Scientific research assures us that myth is not merely a story told but a reality lived; it is not an idle tale, but an active force in human living. It not only represents a vital meaning for a people, but gives a cultural and social coherence to a people whose unity would disintegrate with the loss of a common mythological heritage. Myth expresses the experience of that which is most sacred and pre-eminently real in the human life-story of individuals and societies. It attempts to express man's position in a mysterious universe, his effort to gain that self- understanding which is inherent in his very mode of existence."[5]

Although there are many voices vouching for the vitality of myth in the life of individuals and society at large, there are still those who, down in history, attacked the accepted explanations of the reality of myth. Among the Greek philosophers we have Heraclitus, Xenophanes and Plato. Among recent scholars, we have E. B. Tylor who explains myth "as a product of the confusion of early humans, mixing together without distinction their dream and waking experience."[6] These category of people denied myth of any truth content or any historical value. But in the religious circle where myth is seen as a sacred narrative and sacred history, as well making manifest hidden truths and facts of life, the story is different. How then, is myth understood or defined religiously?

Myth and Religion:

Ninian Smart, in his study of the nature of religion, identified seven dimensions of religion. One of these dimensions is the mythic dimension, which he described as:

> The story side of religion. It is typical of all faiths to hand vital stories: some historical; some about that mysterious primordial time when the world was in its timeless dawn; . . . some about great founders, such as Moses, the Buddha, Jesus, and Muhammad . . . These stories are often called myths . . . in the context of the modern study of religion there is no implication that a myth is false. [7]

Myth, as we have already seen, has its social, historical, cultural, religious, and psychological aspects, but it is religion that popularizes myth today. Accordingly, Honko believed firmly that myth, which he understood as a story of the gods, and a religious account of the beginnings, is brought to life within the context of religious rituals, dances, celebrations, and arts. Ritual brings the creative events of the beginning of time to life and enables them to be repeated here and now, in the present.[8] Without religion myth perhaps would not attract the much attention that is giving to it with the academic circle. Hence most people defines myth strictly from it religious aspect. For example, Anthony Thiselton, has this to say in his definition of myth: "Strictly the term (myth) denotes stories or narratives told about God or divine beings, narrated in a communal setting as of permanent significance, and believed to be true within the community in question."[9]

The Essence of Myth in Religion.

Everything that religion stands and strives upon has a mythical background. Religion in its totality revolves around myth. From the stories of its founder, the world views, stories of the beginnings, end time stories, basic beliefs and doctrines, and even ethical and morals norms are mythical. It is rightly observed by Hopfe and Woodward, that,

> One of the most common characteristics of all religions, basic and advanced, is mythology. In preliterate societies, especially, a religion is sustained and explained by the transmission of its myths from one generation to the next. Religious myths often are used to explain the whys and hows of the world."[10]

It is in myth (as stories and narratives) that religion expresses itself. As expressed by Smart, "The Christian Mass or communion service, for instance, commemorates and presents the story of the Last Supper . . . The Jewish Passover ceremonies commemorates and make real to us the event of the Exodus from Egypt . . ."[11]

Myth makes the distant past present and closer to religious devotees and worshippers. Through rituals and celebrations, it keeps their faith alive. According to Parrinder, "The dramas of ritual express the myth or sacred story which is celebrated at intervals. There are myths of many kinds: of creation, divine example, renewal, construction, initiation and the eternal life. Myths of the creation of the world or the renewal of vegetation are enacted at the new year and at harvest."[12]. Expressed in another way, it is "by acting out the myths, that the devotees of the religion identify with the divine characters and their actions . . . Often, religious rituals re-enact mythologies."[13]

Within the celebration of rituals and other ceremonies, it is myth that defines who performs which function and why such rituals are observed in a particular day other than other days. The explanation of Hopfe and Woodward is very insightful here:

> Myth also may explain the power of certain religious functionaries. The Japanese myth of the sun goddess Amaterasu gives background to the belief that the emperor is a divine figure. Often, myths are attached to and explain why the worshipping community keeps certain religious holy days.[14]

Another area of religion that myth plays a very significant role is doctrinal instruction and education. This aspect is very prominent in tribal religions like African Traditional Religion. Not being a religion of the books, African Traditional Religion uses mainly narratives and myths in passing religious ideas, beliefs, and practices from one generation to another. In the words of E. Eze, "Myths in African Traditional Religion are popular method of education: they communicate religious knowledge and morality while amusing or frightening those who hear or read them.[15]

CONCLUSION.
This study so far has reviewed the relationship between religion and myth, and the essence of myth in religion. Myth plays a very

central role in religion as an institution, and in the belief and faith life of the religious adherent. For instance, it is myth that explains the significance of ritual actions. It is myth that brings the life and experiences of religious founders and ancestors. It is myth that transmits religious doctrines and myth that explains how and why ethical norms came to be. It is myth that tells how society evolves, and why a place has more religious significance than others do.

Notes.

1. G. A. Gaskell, *Dictionary of all Scriptures and Myths.* (New York: Gramercy Books, 1960), 522.
2. William L. Reese, *Dictionary of Philosophy and Religion.* (New York: Humanity Books, 1999), 503.
3. Alan Dundes, Ed., *Sacred Narratives: Readings in the Theory of Myth.* (Los Angeles: University of California Press, 1984), 47-49.
4. Ibid., 198.
5. John Navone, *Seeking God in Story.* (Minnesota: The Liturgical Press, 1990), 56-57
6. William L. Reese, *Dictionary of Philosophy and Religion,* 503.
7. Gary E. Kessler, *Philosophy of Religion: Towards a Global Perspective,* (California: Wadsworth Publishing Company, 1999), 5
8. Alan Dundes, Ed., *Sacred Narratives: Readings in the Theory of myth,* 49-51.
9. Anthony C. Thiselton, *A Concise Encyclopedia of the Philosophy of Religion.* (Michigan: Baker Academic, 2002), 193.
10. Lewis M. Hopfe and Mark R. Woodward, *Religions of the World, 8ᵗʰ ed.* (New Jersey: Prentice Hall, 2001), 25.
11. Gary E. Kessler, *Philosophy of Religion: Towards a Global Perspective,* 6.
12. Geoffrey Parrinder, *World Religions: From Ancient History to the Present.* (New York: Fact On File Inc., 1985), 20.
13. Hopfe and Woodward, *Religions of the World,* 26 Ibid., 25.
14. E. C. Eze, "Religion and Philosophy" in *World Era Encyclopedia* vol. 10, Edited by Pierre-Damien Mvuyekure (New York: Thomas-Gale, 2003), 274

6.2 COSMIC MYTHS IN JUDEO-CHRISTIAN RELIGIONS VIS-A-VIS TRIBAL RELIGIONS: A COMPARATIVE ANALYSIS.

Introduction.

The study of myth and mythology covers a wide range of scholarship. Hence, some modern scholars have come to classify myth into four categories according to theme and genre. The four dominant categories of myth and mythological themes are: cosmic myths, theistic myths, hero or personality myths, and place or event myths. Our concern in this paper, however, is on one of these genres, namely cosmic myths, (which some scholars, like Eliade, called cosmogonic myths), especially as they appear in the Judeo-Christian religions and Tribal religions. In dealing with this, we shall not dwell on the vast cosmic mythological themes in these religions, as that alone would form a doctoral dissertation. Consequently, I will limit myself only to certain aspect of these themes, namely, the myths of the origin of things (creation), and the myths of the origin of death. The essence of this paper is to draw a comparative analysis of these stories or myths as they occur in these religions.

Cosmic Myths: A Definition.

Cosmic myths literarily are myths that tell about the creation of the world, mysterious primordial times, and the end of the world. They also indicate how death came into the world. Ancient and tribal religions are full of myths of this nature. The oldest of such myths according to recorded history are probably those of Egypt in North Africa, and the Babylonian story of the Enuma elish and the Epic of Gilgamesh.[1] We also find such myths in Judeo-Christian religions, African traditional religions, and Islam, among other religions.

Mircea Eliade defined cosmic or cosmogonic myth (a term he preferred to use) as:

> the central myth which describes the beginning of the
> world that is what happened before the world became as

it is today . . . a cosmogonic myth . . . describes the first germinal stage of the world. This beginning is always implied in the sequence of myths, which recounts the fabulous event that took place after the creation or the coming into being of the universe, namely, the myths of the origin of plants, animals, and man, or even the origin of marriage, family, and death, etc. Taken all together, these myths of origin constitute a fairly coherent history. They reveal how the cosmos was shaped and changed, how man became mortal, sexually diversified, and compelled to work in order to live; they equally reveal what the supernatural beings and the mythical ancestors did, and how and why they abandoned the earth and disappeared.[2]

Hence, cosmic myths are concerned with the world and how it is ordered. Nearly all mythologies of the world have story about creation. Cosmic myth is sometimes called cosmogony, which literally means "birth of the world."[3]

Cosmic Myths in Judeo-Christian.

Judeo-Christian religions are full of many cosmic themes that are recorded both in the Old Testament and New Testament. Among such themes are the origin of the world, humanity, plants, aquatic life and other living and non living things; the origin of death, evil and sufferings; and the end of world. As I mentioned at the introduction, we shall limit ourselves to the cosmic myths of creation and death as recorded in the book of Genesis 1-3, which both Christians and Jews regard as authoritative and fundamental to their faiths.

The first chapters of the book of Genesis, namely, Chapters 1-11 are primordial history; they introduce the reader to the story (myth) of salvation, the theme that runs through the whole Bible. They search back into the origin of the world and survey the whole human race. According to Thompson, "They (Gen. 1-11) tell of the creation of the universe and man, of the fall and its consequences (suffering and death), of the increasing human wickedness (evil) which earned the punishment of the flood."[4]

In the book of Genesis, they are two different myths or stories of creation. In the first, God created everything *ex nihilo*, (out of nothing) for a period of seven days. In the second, they are primary (things created out nothing), and secondary creation (things created out of something already existing, e.g. man from dust, and woman from man). Let us briefly look at these stories from the Bible. "In the beginning God created the heaven and earth. Now the earth was a formless void, there was darkness over the deep, and God's spirit hovered over the water. God said, let there be light and there was light . . . let there be a vault in the water to divided waters into two. Therefore, it was . . . God said, let us make man in our own image. God created man in the image of himself, male and female he created them . . . On the seventh day God completed all the work he had been doing . . . Such were the origins of heaven and earth when they were created."[5] This is a summary of first story of creation. The second story goes this way,

> At the time when God made heaven and earth, there was as yet no wild bush on the earth nor had any wild plant yet sprung up, nor was there any man to till the soil . . . God fashioned man of the dust from the soil. Then he breathed into his nostril a breath of life, and thus man became a living being . . . God said it is not good for man to be alone . . . so God made the man fall into a deep sleep. And while he slept, he took one of his ribs and enclosed it in flesh. He built the rib into a woman, and brought her to the man.[6]

The above quotations summarize the myth of the origin of the world and everything therein. Another cosmic myth that is of importance in the central teachings of Judeo-Christian religions is the myth of the origin of death and evil. This myth relates that suffering and death originated with the disobedience and fall of Eve and Adam who succumbed to the Serpent's (Devil) temptation by eating the forbidden fruit. The book of Genesis chapter three has it that, "But of the fruit of the tree in the middle of the garden God said, 'you shall must not eat it, nor touch it, under pain of death . . . The woman saw that the tree was good to eat and pleasing to the eyes . . . she took some of its fruit and ate it. She gave some also to her husband who was with her, and he ate it. (As a punishment God said), with your sweat on your brow shall you eat bread, until you return to the soil, as you were taken from it. For dust you are and to dust you shall return."[7] Accepting this myth as the origin of death, the New Testament stated, "Sin entered the world through one man, and through sin death, and thus death has spread through the whole human race because everyone has sinned . . . Death reigned over all from Adam."[8]

The above two myths describe the creation by God at the beginning of time, God's special intervention in the making of man and woman, the unity of the human race, the sin of the first parents, the fall from divine favor and the penalties (suffering and death) they and their descendants would inherit in consequence of the sin.

Cosmic Myths in Tribal Religions.

Scarcely is there any tribe that does not have cosmic mythological themes in their religion and or culture. The cosmic myths of Africans are as varied as the many cultures which inhabit the continent. Cosmogony mythologies play an important role in West African societies; they set up the framework of the social, political, and even economic structure of society.[9] In this section of our paper, we shall limit ourselves to one tribe, namely the Yoruba tribe of Southwestern Nigeria.

Among the Yoruba of southwestern Nigeria, the story about the creation of the world at Ile-Ife, the location of a small but famous city, has become a widely known account. According to Bolaji Idowu:

> In the beginning, there was only the creator God, Olodumare, who lived in the sky, and the earth below, which was covered by the primordial waters. After

creating the gods, called orisha, Olodumare told one them to take a container of earth and spread it out over the waters to create more dry land. According to the divination poems, Olodumare originally gave the task of creation to Obatala. He became drunk on palm wine when he arrived on the earth and forgot his mission, so Olodumare delegated the task to Odudua. Odudua came down from the sky by means of iron chains that hung down to the earth.[10]

Having created the earth, the next task was to populate it with human beings and other living things. As related by Benjamin C. Ray, "The other deities followed Odudua to the earth. Olodumare gave to Obatala the task of creating the first human beings at Ile-Ife by shaping them from clay into which Olodumare placed the breath of life. Henceforth, Obatala became the creator of human beings. He shapes them in the womb, and Olodumare provides the life-breath. Because of Obatala's tendency to become drunk on palm wine, he sometimes creates human beings with physical deformities, and these become his devotees, who worship him at his shrines."[11]

When the whole of creation was complete, Olodumare withdrew from the earth because of a quarrel that occurred between the sky and the earth. Although he withdrew from the earth, he remained the Supreme God. According to Joseph Omoyajowo, "Olodumare reigns supreme in the distant sky and rules the world through his intermediaries, the orisha. The sky dwelling Olodumare is transcendent, all-knowing, and all powerful. Unlike orisha, he has no temples or priests, and no sacrifices or offerings are made to him because his will cannot be influenced or changed. Yet, Olodumare may be invoked by anyone, anywhere, at any time to give him praise and him know of their needs."[12]

A Comparative Analysis of Cosmic Myths in Judeo-Christian Religion and Tribal Religion.

We have presented the mythical themes of the creation of the world and its content, and the origin of death in Judeo-Christian religions, and in the Yoruba tribe of Nigeria. A closer look at these stories reveals an interesting relationship.

Both stories of creation contain a separation motif. There is a separation of heaven (sky) and earth, there is a separation between waters and land, and there is also a separation between the creator and the creature. In both stories, the creator after creating retires to a distant and isolated heaven or sky. Analyzing the creation story of Genesis, Madison Bell observed, "Creation according to Genesis is a story of separation and division. In the very beginning, God stands separate from the formless materials which the cosmos is to be made, and at end, when His speech has divided everything into its proper category, God remains apart from His creation and in some sense remote from it."[13] The observation of Bell regarding the story of Genesis is also very correct of the Yoruba story.

Again, both myths have the concept of the primordial water covering the whole earth. In both stories, man is fashioned from dust, and life came to the man as gift of breath from the creator.

Another thing common in the both religions is the concept or death. In the Yoruba tribe, death came about not from God but because of the distraction, man caused the dog that was to present the wish of life to God. While the dog was distracted by the smell of delicious meat, the tortoise, with the wish of death out ran him and presented death to God before the arrival of the dog. In this story, God (Olodumare), is not blamable for death, just like in the story of Genesis, it is Adam and Eve, not God that brought death to themselves through their disobedience.

Conclusion.

Do we conclude that the Yoruba myth of creation which has much literary and structural resemblance with the creation myth in book of Genesis was influenced by the latter? The answer is no. The Yoruba story is independent of the Genesis story. Yoruba land has no geographical relationship or proximity with world of Genesis. Again, before the coming of Christianity to Yoruba land, the story has been part of oral tradition for many centuries. Hence, we can conclude that both are different stories with coincidental resemblances. While we acknowledge their resemblance, we must also acknowledge that the theology behind them is quite different. While the cosmic myth of Judeo-Christian religions presents a monotheistic creator God, the cosmic myth of tribal (Yoruba) religion presents a polytheistic god, who created and rules the world with and through his intermediaries – the gods, deities and other spirits.

Notes.

1. H.W. F. Saggs, *The Babylonians*. (London: Macmillan Publishers Ltd, 1988), 309.
2. Alan Dundes, Ed., *Sacred Narrative: Readings in the Theory of Myth*. (Los Angeles: Univ. of California Press, 1984), 141-2.
3. *Cosmic Myths* http://www.geocities.com/folk_king2003/cosmic (accessed February 20, 2008)
4. Thomas L. Thompson, *The Mythic Past: Biblical Archeology and the Myth of Israel*. (London: Random House, 1999), 82.
5. Genesis 1: 1 – 2:4; Matthew 19: 4.
6. Genesis 2:5-23.
7. Genesis 3:3-7, 19.
8. Romans 5:12-14.
9. John Mbiti, "General Manifestations of African Religiosity" http://www.afrikaworld.net/afrel/mbiti.htm (accessed February 20, 2008)
10. E. Bolaji Idowu, *Olodumare: God in Yoruba Belief*. (London: Longmans, 1962), 19.
11. Benjamin C. Ray, *African Religions: Symbol, Ritual and Community*. (New Jersey: Prentice Hall, 2000), 9.
12. Jacob k. Olupona, Ed., *African Traditional Religions in Contemporary Society*. (New York: Paragon House, 1991), 76.
13. David Rosenberg, Ed., *Genesis As It Is Written*. (San Francisco: HarperCollins Publishers, 1996), 28.

6.3 THE NEW TESTAMENT GOSPEL MESSAGE AS A MYTH.

Introduction.

To a fundamentalist and a "Bible only" believing Christian, to suggest that the New Testament gospel message, which is the story of the life and teachings Jesus, is a "myth" is to utter blasphemy punishable in hell fire. To a non-Christian such a statement will be welcomed as it suggests to him or her that the Christian message is false and not to be trusted. As expressed by John Shelby Spong, "The suggestion that the key elements of a faith tradition have been caught up in and are interpreted by the mythological patterns of the ages disturbs some people, even while it promises new insights for others."[1] The reason for the above-mentioned attitudes is that the word *myth* has been erroneously taken to mean "falsehood" or "false teaching," when applied to religious beliefs and doctrines. As a result, no one would want to associate the word myth to the sacred text of his religion. Other people scriptures could be myths, but not one's own. As Joseph Campbell observed, "most people have no difficulty seeing the mythological elements in a religious system other than their own."[2]

What does it actually mean to say that the New Testament gospel message is a myth? Does it mean that the whole content and foundation of the Christian faith is false and fictitious? To what extent is the gospel message historical and true? These are some of the questions that this paper will address.

Explication of Terms.

To put this essay in its proper perspective and to prompt a better understanding, it is important that we begin by clarifying the key terms or concepts that are involved, namely, the New Testament, the gospel message, and myth. Understanding these three terms will guide our understanding of how the New Testament gospel message is and is not a myth.

i. **The New Testament:** The New Testament occupies a place of primary importance in the lives of Christians. It is to taken to be the direct words of Jesus and or his immediate disciples. According to Ringer, "The New Testament books were written 45-95 A.D"[3] The New Testament was not thrown down from heaven as a complete book. The twenty seven books that make up of what we have today as the New Testament, has a long history. As recorded in the *New Advent Catholic Encyclopedia*:

> The New Testament was not written all at once. The books that compose it appeared one after another in the space of fifty years, i.e. in the second half of the first century. Written in different and distant countries and addressed to particular Churches, they took some time to spread throughout the whole of Christendom, and a much longer time to become accepted. The unification of the canon was not accomplished without much controversy. Still it can be said that from the third century, or perhaps earlier, the existence of all the books that today form our New Testament was everywhere known, although they were not all universally admitted, at least as certainly canonical. However, uniformity existed in the West from the fourth century. The East had to await the seventh century to see an end to all doubts on the subject.[4]

It is obvious from the above quotation that what we have as the New Testament came out of already existing stories that form part of general oral traditions. These stories are what in the religious context are called mythologies. Some of the stories that form part of the New Testament Scripture were already known ancient in pre-Christian mythologies, as we shall later in this paper.

ii. The Gospel Message: The gospel message falls within the corpus of work that is today called the story or the tale of Jesus. Put in another way, the story or tale Jesus can be called the myth of Jesus who is called the Christ.

Etymologically, the word "gospel" has an Anglo-Saxon root. Accordingly, "The English language, gospel represents Middle

English terminology derived from the Old English *godspel* (from *god*, "good," and *spel* "story"). Gospel is the common translation of the Late Latin *evangelium*, which is a virtual transliteration of the Greek *euaggelion* . . . In the Septuagint (a Greek translation of he Hebrew scripture) the verb *euaggelizien* specially connotes the announcement of the good news of salvation."[5]

In its pagan usage, prior to its adoption as a Christian term, gospel designates the story of victory, and the principal events of the life of the Emperor, who was a god and savior.[6] These stories and announcements of victory and events all have mythological themes, especially themes that presented the rulers as half-human and half-divine.

The New Testament gospel, strictly, speaking refers to the gospels according to Matthew, Mark, Luke, and John, respectively. Nevertheless, broadly speaking, it covers the whole the economy of salvation as recorded in the New Testament. The stories that came to be collated into what is now called the Gospels in the New Testament, like other mythological stories, first circulated among the community as part of the oral tradition. They were committed into memory, preserved and transmitted from one generation to another as sacred story (myths). Stressing more on this, Kelber says, "Speaking was undoubtedly a primary means of keeping the memory of Jesus alive. But what kind of Jesus was it who was remembered in the stories and sayings? The early Christian had penchant for storytelling . . ."[7] Obviously, the stories and sayings of Jesus were what popularly became the kerygma that centers not primarily on the historical Jesus but on his deeds of redemption and salvation. This kerygma, which is mythological in content, is what we call today "the gospel message." It was this message that Paul proclaimed, not based on his historical knowledge of Jesus but on what was handed down in oral tradition.

The gospel message is therefore the story of Jesus as told by the early Christian Church, a story, which is myth. The question then is, what do we mean by myth?

iii. Myth: The word "myth" and what it stands for has been variously defined and interpreted by scholars within various texts and contexts without any general consensus. Etymologically, the word "myth" is derived, from "the Greek term *mythos* meaning 'legend.' Hence a narrative account taken to true, but not known to be true."[8] The word *mythos* has other connotations outside legend. It is also stands for stories, sayings, and tales that encompass everything we can possibly think of, ranging from the sacred down to the profane, from the ordinary to the mysterious, and from the physical to the spiritual. Based on classical mythological distinctions, myth refers to tales of the gods, while legend refers to tales of human heroes.

Drawing from the above understanding of myth, Lauri Honko articulated twelve ways by which myth can be described or understood, namely: myth as source of cognitive categories, myth as form of symbolic expression, myth as projection of the subconscious, myth as an integrating factor in man's adaptation to life, myth as character of behavior, myth as legitimization of social institutions, myth as mirror of culture and social structure, myth as result of historical situation, myth as religious communication, myth as religious genre, and myth as medium for structure.[9]

Generally, myth has been defined simply as story, narrative, or even fiction. But it goes beyond a mere story. In the words of Malinowski:

> Myth as it exists in a salvage community that is in its living primitive form, is not merely a story told but a reality lived. It is not of the nature of fiction, such as we read today in a novel, but it is a living reality believed to have once happened in primeval times, and continuing ever since to influence the world and human destinies. This myth is to the savage what, to a fully believing Christian, is the Biblical story of Creation, of the Fall, of Redemption by Christ's sacrifice on the Cross.[10]

Following the same line of thought as Malinowski's, Navone, said, "Scientific research assures us that myth is not merely a story told but a reality lived; it is not an idle tale, but an active force in human living. It not only represents a vital meaning for a people, but gives a cultural and social coherence to a people whose unity would disintegrate with the loss of a common mythological heritage. Myth expresses the experience of that which is most sacred and pre-eminently real in the human life-story of individuals and societies. It attempts to express man's position in a mysterious universe, his effort to gain that self—understanding which is inherent in his very mode of existence."[11]

From the above description of myth, we can see that the gospel message falls within the category of what is today called myth: a living reality believed to have once happened in primeval times, and continuing ever since to influence the world and human destinies.

The Mythic Content of the Gospel Message.

Ninian Smart, in his study of the nature of religion, identified seven dimensions of religion. Among these dimensions is the mythic dimension, which he described as:

> The story side of religion. It is typical of all faiths to hand vital stories: some historical; some about that mysterious primordial time when the world was in its timeless dawn; . . . some about great founders, such as Moses, the Buddha, Jesus, and Muhammad . . . These stories are often called myths . . . in the context of the modern study of religion there is no implication that a myth is false. [12]

The gospel message typically falls within the above quotation. It developed out of mythological tradition and flourished within such traditions. This is typical of all religions. According to Spong, "Religious traditions are strange combinations of subjective descriptions of actual events plus mythological interpretations of those events. It is only when an actual event enters into and is carried by a mythological interpretations that the event is fully remembered at all. Whatever it was that resided in the moment when Christianity was born had to been caught up in a mythological framework almost at once or it would have perished. Legends, symbols, and myths gathered around the moment, as they do whenever time and eternity appear to intersect."[13]

The gospel story was largely influenced by pre-Christian mythologies, which were later incorporated into the corpus of the gospel. The presence of these mythological stories,

> Where designed to capture the meaning of both the origin and the destiny of Jesus of Nazareth, who was cast as the mythic hero. The dominant myth of his origin was expressed in the story of the virgin birth – a theme that has repeated countless times in almost every religious system, from Zoroaster to Romulus and Remus. The ultimate destiny of this Jesus was portrayed in the mythological account of his return to God in a cosmic ascension, another theme that is quite popular in many religious traditions.[14]

Commenting further on the gospel narrative or story of Jesus as a Christian myth that has some connection with other non-Christian mythologies, Robertson said:

> The Christian myth grew by absorbing details from pagan cults. The birth story is similar to many nativity myths in the pagan world. The Christ had to have a Virgin for a mother. Like the image of the child-god in the cult of Dionysus, he was pictured in swaddling clothes in a basket manger. He was born in a stable like Horus—the stable temple of the Virgin Goddess, Isis, Queen of heaven. Again, like Dionysus, he turned water into wine; like Aesculapius, he raised men from the dead and gave sight to the blind; and like Attis and Adonis, he is mourned and rejoiced over by women. His resurrection took place, like that of Mithras, from a rock tomb.[15]

Another mythic content of the gospel is the Eucharistic or the Last Supper myth. Like the other myths already alluded to, it has an influence of other mythical themes. This influence is unavoidable because, as Starwyn noted, "No religion developed in a vacuum. All religions are influenced not only by its predecessors but by the contemporaries of the time also . . . The Eucharist goes back into history and is based upon the ritual consumption of the God man. Osiris, Dionysus, Attis and many other were ritually consumed."[16]

Another mythical content of the gospel is the parable discourses. Most of the sayings and teachings of Jesus were in parables. According to the Gospel of Mark, "Using many parables, like these he spoke the word to them, so far as they were capable of understanding it. He would not speak except in parables"[17] The question we need to ask is, what is a parable?

According to the *New Advent Catholic Encyclopedia,* "The word *parable* (Hebrew *mashal*; Syrian *mathla*, Greek *parabole*) signifies, in general, a comparison, or a parallel, by which one thing is used to illustrate another. It is a likeness taken from the sphere of real, or sensible, or earthly incidents, in order to convey an ideal, or spiritual, or heavenly meaning. As uttering one thing and signifying something else, it is in the nature of a riddle (Hebrew *khidah*, Gr. *ainigma* or *problema*)."[18] The word parable has the following synonyms: allegory, myth, story, fable, legend, tale, lesson, and teaching.[19]

From the above definition and synonyms of parable, we can easily see that greater part of sayings and teachings of Jesus, as recorded in the gospel fall within the context of myth. Such mythical or parabolic passages have no relationship or connection with historical facts at all, but they are real and true when applied to real life situations. It will be absurd and a waste of time to go Jerusalem or Jericho and start looking for the spot or the hospital where the wounded traveler in the parable of the Good Samaritan (Luke 10: 29-37) was taken to. The story is a myth, and there are many of such parabolic-myths in the gospel. In line with this understanding, scholars like John R. Donahue, summarized the gospel as "narrative parable of the meaning of the life and death of Jesus."[20] Expressing the same view, John Dominic Crossan said, "Jesus announced the kingdom of God in parables, but the primitive church announced Jesus as Christ, the parable of God."[21]

The "Mythic" Gospel: True, Fact or False?

Having established that the gospel message is a myth, do we, then, mean to say that the gospel is false? Definitely, no. As rightly observed by Smart, the term myth may be a bit misleading and often time misinterpreted as false, but in the context of the modern study of religion there is no implication that a myth is false.[22] Do we, then, mean that the gospel is literarily true, historical, and factual? The answer is no. What, then, do we mean?

In discussing the veracity or truthfulness of myth, Russell Kirk stated that, "mythical expression in literature is intended to wake us from inattention to important human truths and values."[23] For the religious believers, the mythical basis of their faith is true. The gospel as a story or message of salvation, though mythical, is true. The truth of the gospel does not lie in its historical accuracy, but in its moral teachings and in the message which the writers intended to communicate. One thing we have to get clear is that the gospel is not a chronological historical account of the life, teachings and messages of Jesus. There are sacred narratives. It is obvious that:

> The biblical writers had no sweep at all of historical times . . . There was for the writers of scripture no communication system beyond the word of mouths. Events were recorded only in the memory of observers. We need to be reminded that even in this modern world with its technological genius, there is still no such thing as "objective" history. Our view of history is shaped by our own national interests, by those who have the power to make their view of life the standard view. If this is so for us, how much less objectivity would be served in the ancient world with its narrow focus, its limited embrace of reality . . . [24]

Another aspect of the gospel that presents it as true is that it represents "reality" when applied to concrete human situation. Discussing the truth that lies behind the gospel story (myth), John Navone said:

> Myth is not merely a story told but a reality lived; it is not an idle tale, but an active force in human living. Myth expresses the experience of that which is most sacred and pre-eminently real in the human life-story of individuals and societies. It attempts to express man's position in a mysterious universe, his effort to gain that self-understanding which is inherent in his very mode of existence.[25]

A typical example is the parable of Good Samaritan, already cited. As mythical as this story is, without any historical or factual basis, it has a truth content of how we should relate to our neighbors and with people far and near. Understanding the truth of most of the stories in the gospel in this sense, David Robert Ord and Robert B. Coote said, "Many biblical stories are like *Animal Farm*. They are true, though not historically accurate or factual. They are concerned with proclaiming a message, not with providing us with a chronology of events from the history of Israel or the life of Jesus of Nazareth. We must learn them not as history but as message."[26]

The gospel myth or story, read and understood as a message, and not historical or literal facts, "implies truth, not falsehood; not primitive, naïve misunderstanding but an insight more profound than scientific description and logical analysis can achieve . . . Myth is recognized as a symbolic expression of truths about man's own life and thought. Myths express man's self-understanding or his groping towards an identity."[27]

Conclusion.

There is no scripture of any religion in the world that is devoid of mythic qualities and materials. Just as there are cultural, psychological and spiritual realities that underlie myth, so also there are religious realties. This religious reality transforms the mythic aspect of any religion, the New Testament gospel inclusive, from the notion of falsehood to an exalted level of a true story; a true story that sustains and nourishes the faith and life of the adherents. But it will be wrong for believers in their in recounting (reading the scriptures) their faith story to look for literary facts is such stories, which play the role of myths. This should be the attitude of all who read the New Testament gospel message.

Notes:
1. John Shelby Spong, *Resurrection: Myth or Reality*. (New York: HarperCollins, 1994), 39-40.
2. Ibid., 39.
3. Wesley Ringer, "History of the Bible: How the Bible Came to Us", in
GodAndScience.org   http://godandscience.org/apologetics/ bibleorigin.html
(accessed on September 20, 2007).
4. *New Advent Catholic Encyclopedia: New Testament* http://www. newadvent.org/cathen/14530a.htm (accessed February 13, 2008).
5. Mircea Eliade, Ed, *Encyclopedia of Religion vol. 6.* (New York: Macmillan
Publishing Company, 1987), 79-80.
6. Xavier Leon-Dufour, *Dictionary of Biblical Theology.* (Boston: Geoffrey
Chapman, 1992), 215.
7. Werner H. Kelber, *The Oral and The Written Gospel.* (Philadelphia: Fortress
Press, 1983), 70.
8. William L. Reese, *Dictionary of Philosophy and Religion.* (New York: Humanity Books, 1999), 503.
9. Alan Dundes, Ed., *Sacred Narrative: Readings in the Theory of Myth.* (Los Angeles: Univ. of California Press, 1984), 47-49.
10. Ibid., 198.

11. John Navone, *Seeking God in Story.* (Minnesota: The Liturgical Press, 1990), 56-57

12. Gary E. Kessler, *Philosophy of Religion: Towards a Global Perspective.* (California: Wadsworth Publishing Company, 1999), 5.

13. John Shelby Spong, *Resurrection: Myth or Reality*, 39.

14. Ibid., 40.

15. J. M. Robertson, *Pagan Christs.* (New York: Barns & Nobles, 1996), 68.

16. Strawyn, "The Christian Myth is almost totally Pagan in Origin." http://www.holysmoke.org/hs02/mithra8.htm (accessed February 27, 2008).

17. Mark 4: 33-34.

18. *New Advent Catholic Encyclopedia: Parable h*ttp://www. newadvent.org/cathen/11460a.htm (accessed February 27, 2008).

19. *Parable. Thesaurus.com.Roget's New Millennium^{TM}*Thesaurus, First Edition (v 1. 3.1) Lexicon Publishing Group, LLC. http://thesaurus.reference.com/browse/parable (February 28, 2008)

20. John R. Donahue, "Jesus as Parable of God in the Gospel of Mark" Int. 32. (1978) 369-86, cited in Werner H. Kelber, *The Oral and The Written Gospel*, 120.

21. John Dominic Crossan, *The Dark Interval: Towards a Theology of Story.* (Illinois: Argus Communication, 1975), 124.

22. Kessler, *Philosophy of Religion*, 5.

23. Russell Kirk, *Enemies of the Permanent Thing.* (New York: Arlington House, 1969), 111.

24. John Shelby Spong, *Rescuing the Bible from Fundamentalism.* (New York: HarperCollins Publishers, 1992), 37.

25. Navone, *Seeking God in Story*, 57.

26. David R. Ord and Robert B. Coote, *Is the Bible True?* (New York: Orbis Books, 1994), 33.

27. Navone, *Seeking God in Story*, 56.

CHAPTER SEVEN

ESSAYS ON PHILOSOPHY OF RELIGION

7.1 THE QUESTION OF RELIGION AND TRUTH: RELIGIOUS RESPONSES TO THE CHALLENGES OF MODERNITY.

Introduction.

The period of Enlightenment in Europe can be described as a period of human's liberation from the dominance of religion, and enthronement of reason in every aspect of human life. With the Enlightenment, the 19th century witnessed a radical critique of religion. Religion was criticized, the foundations of faith were questioned, and God was "attacked." Filled with the spirit of that period, Marx said, "For Germany, the criticism of religion is in the main complete, and criticism of religion is the premise of all criticism."[1]

The Enlightenment was the dawn of modernity and its ancillaries namely: secularism, science, technology, etc. Prior to this period, religion was the ultimate source of truth. The Enlightenment challenged and questioned the authority of religion on matters of truth. As expressed by Shenk, "Prior to the Enlightenment, the Church and faith were the soul of culture; this was the way of life. The Enlightenment changed all of that by giving faith and church a label – Religion . . . Enlightenment thinkers believed that reason rather than religion needed to be arbiter of self-evident morality and truth."[2]

Thus, modernity sought to replace religious world-view of faith, belief, spirituality, morality, and values with skepticism, secularism, humanism, pluralism, consumerism, social materialism, excessive interest in human sexuality. The modern world-view replaced religion as the source of truth with science, empiricism, and rationality.

Our concern in this essay is to investigate the place of religion today in relation to truth amidst the challenges of modernity. Our discussion will center more on the question of truth as it concerns religion and science, a major characteristic of modernity.

What Is Truth?

To put this essay in its proper context, one cannot escape asking one basic question: what is truth? A proper hermeneutics of truth will assists us to know whether there is only one or dual realms of truth, whether such realm or realms are limited to religion alone or to science alone, or to both. It will also help us to consider whether truth resides only in the phenomenal world or extends to the noumenal world.

Truth, like religion, has no universally agreed definition. Throughout human intellectual history, various theories have been proposed as to what constitutes the truth of a matter. The basic theories of truth include:

> The correspondence theory – the true corresponds to reality. The coherence theory – the true is the coherent system of ideas. The pragmatic theory – the true is the workable or satisfactory solution of a problematic situation. The semantic theory – assertions about truth are in a metalanguage and apply to statements of base language. The performative theory – the assertion of truth is the performative act of agreeing with a given statement.[3]

From the above quotation, it is clear that truth does not reside only in one realm, and that there is not one means of realizing or knowing the truth. The correspondent theorists relate truth to reality. Reality is not only in here, but also out there. This favors a stand on religious truth. The coherent theory can be defined as a truth of logic. This notion of truth can be shared by both science and religion. The pragmatic theory is based on the fact of a concrete situation, experientially and experimentally scrutinized. This view may deny religion any access to the truth because most of religious ideas and concepts are not observable and cannot be reduced to experimentation.

Religion and science in today's modern world believe that there is TRUTH, and both lay claim to it, and rightly so. However, the conflict between the truth of religion and the truth of science lies in what is the center and source of truth. For religion, especially theistic religions, it is God. For science, it is human reason. Put in the words of Shenk, "[For Church] there is a center toward which all data points, truth in which reality converges. That center is God. He is the source of all truth, and therefore all reality is touched with meaning and purpose. The Enlightenment agreed with the church that there is a truth center. However, the Enlightenment placed human reason, not God, in that truth center . . . By enthroning human reason, the Enlightenment nudged God into the periphery of reality." This is typical of modernity; religion is placed at the periphery of society.

It is evident from our discussion so far, that there are different realms of truth, and that TRUTH is bigger than religion as it is also bigger than science, that is to say, religion and science may have the truth, but none of them claims to have all the truth. There are truths known to religion that are not known to the sciences, and vice versa. It is also important to note that there is a distinction between truth and fact. According to Raman, "A truth is the interpretation and apprehension of a fact. What this means is that truth is very much a function of the state of the mind that interprets the fact. Thus one might say: Facts are what there seem to be; Truths are how they seem to me. Given that truth is the apprehension of a fact, the same may appear as different truths to different individuals."[5]

In order to define truth as it concerns science and religion in the modern world, Raman insists that:

> The distinction between fact and truth is of utmost importance in any discussion on science and religion. Those who argue that science alone leads to correct knowledge tend to forget that science is essentially an interpenetration of facts. On the other hand, those who insist that religion provides us with ultimate answers as to the nature of the world and of human existence tend to imagine that the truth which religion proclaims is a true reflection of how the world is. Put differently, the world of science tends to equate fact with truth, while the world of religion tends to truth with fact.[6]

Having established, at least to reasonable extent, a proper understanding of truth as it relates to religion in a science-oriented modern world, the big question now is: can religious truth and scientific truth coexist? This is the big challenge. How do religious people face this challenge, and what is the response of scientists to this issue?

Religious Truth and Modernity (Scientific Truth): Any Synthesis?

In today's modern world, there is so much emphasis on the importance of science as the ultimate source of truth. What used to be held as truth religiously has been relegated to the realm of myth; myth in its irreligious understanding of something that is a false and cooked up story. As a result, many people are becoming increasing irreligious. However, some scholars and scientists see such notion of truth lying only within the realm of science as a false notion of science. Hence, there is a new and an increasing awareness of religion and science possessing truth in their fullness in the modern world, though from different perspectives or realms. A unified and authentic system of truth, therefore, is that which combines religious and scientific truth. According to Elder, "Man is as it were, a creature with two eyes . . . One eye looks towards the material world with which science deals; the other towards the world of spiritual values which is the home religion."[7]

Again, to address the question of religion and truth versus modernity/science, we must understand the essential character of religion and the essential character of science. What truth content does religion address and what truth content does science address? Responding to character of religion and science as it relates to truth, Masao Abe said:

> At the risk of oversimplification, one may say that science is concerned with the answer to the question "how" whereas religion is concern with the answer to the question "why." As used here, "how" refers to the process of cause and effect or "means" while "why" refers to meaning, purpose, or *raison d'être*. Science can provide an answer to the question of how a flower blooms, or how man comes to exist. It cannot, however, give an answer to question of why a flower blooms or why man comes to exist. It can explain the cause of a given a fact but not the meaning or ground of the fact. It is religion, not science that can offer an answer to the question "why."[8]

The above quotation reveals that they are two indispensible realms of truth: religious and scientific.

Albert Einstein, one of the founding fathers of modern science opined that the scientific spirit is itself religious. He said, "But science can only be created by those who are thoroughly imbued with the aspiration toward truth and understanding. This source of feeling, however, springs from the sphere of religion. To this there also belongs the faith in the possibility that the regulations valid for the world of existence are rational, that is, comprehensible to reason. I cannot conceive of a genuine scientist without that profound faith. The situation may be expressed by an image: science without religion is lame, religion without science is blind."[9] Einstein, a renowned scientist, believed that there are truths that lie outside the scope of science, and resides within the domain of religion. Accordingly, he said in 1948, "While it is true that science, to the extent of its grasp of causative connections, may reach important conclusions as to the compatibility and incompatibility of goals and evaluations, the independent and fundamental definitions regarding goals and values remain beyond science's reach."[10]

The dialogue between Mathieu Ricard, a Buddhist monk and Trinh Xuan Thuan, a scientist, in *The Quantum and the Lotus*, reveals a striking synthesis between science and religion. The scientist, Thuan, in his conclusion said there is a definite convergence and resonance between the Buddhist and scientific visions of reality. Some of Buddhism's views on the world of phenomena are strikingly similar to the underlying notions of modern physics even though Buddhism and science have radically different ways of investigating the nature of reality, this does not lead to an inseparable opposition, but rather to a harmonious complementarily. That is because both are on quests for the truth, and both use criteria of authenticity, rigor, and logic. So reality can be perceived in various ways, and different approaches – one turned inward and the outward – can lead to the same truths.[11] Buddhism as non-theistic religion, through its concepts of dependent co-origination, Emptiness and Suchness offers a view of religious truth very much compatible with modern scientific truth. This is so because scientific truth presents a truth of an impersonal world. Similarly, the above-mentioned Buddhist concepts are also somewhat impersonal and at the same time deeply religious.

The official teaching of the Catholic Church, as enunciated by Vatican II, is that scientific truth complements religious truth and vice versa. However, the Church honestly admits that modernity poses a serious challenge to religion. In the *Gaudiun et Spes,* the fathers of the Second Vatican Council admit that the scientific spirit has a new kind of impact on the cultural sphere and on modes of thought. Technology is now transforming the face of the earth, and is already trying to master outer space. To a certain extent, the human intellect is also broadening its dominion over time. These new conditions have their impact on religion. Growing numbers of people are abandoning religion in practice. Nevertheless, in the face of the modern development of the world, the number constantly swells of the people who raise the most basic questions about life; questions whose truth lie outside the scope of science, and which religion alone can give satisfactory answer.[12] In the words of Cardinal Paul Poupard, head of the Pontifical Council for Culture, the faithful should listen to what secular modern science has to offer, for religion risks turning into "fundamentalism" if it ignores scientific reason.[13]

To objectively perceive reality as it is in today's modern world, we need the truth of science and the truth of religion. Science identifies truth as it appears within the observable world of phenomena, and nothing more than that. Religion on the hand transcends the phenomenal world to the noumenal realm. Einstein believed and maintained that there are truths that the knowledge of science alone cannot reveal to the modern world. For such truth to be accessible we need religion. In 1939, he said that the scientific method can teach us nothing else beyond how facts are related to, and conditioned by, each other. Objective knowledge provides us with powerful instruments for the achievements of certain ends. To make clear these fundamental ends and valuations, and to set them fast in the emotional life of the individual, he assumed, is precisely the most important function which religion has to perform in the social life of man. And if one asks whence derives the authority of such fundamental ends, since they cannot be stated and justified merely by reason, one can only answer: They come into being not through demonstration but through revelation.[14]

Invariably, the modern man cannot lay claim to a holistic truth without a proper synthesis of scientific truth and religious truth. I wish to conclude this section with these beautiful words of Masao Abe, "Science without religion is dangerous, for it necessarily entails a complete mechanization of humanity. On the other hand, religion without science is powerless in that it lacks an effective means by which to actualize religious meaning in the contemporary world."[15]

The Relevance of Religious Truth in the Scientific Modern World.

In his discussion on the relevance of religious truth in the modern world, Varadaraja V. Raman distinguishes two types of truth: ***Exopotent*** and ***Endopotent*** truths. Exopotent is the truth of science, while endopotent is the truth of religion. The modern society needs both of them on an equal basis. As Raman puts it, "A scientific truth can and often does have consequences (impacts) on our understanding and manipulation of the external world. We may say that scientific truths are exopotent. Exopotent truths are fruitful, i.e. they lead to useful/practical applications. A religious truth can have consequences (impacts) on our internal experience of life as individuals, especially in the context of our particular circumstances. We may say that religious Endopotent truths are fulfilling, i.e. they lead to psychologically/emotionally satisfying consequences."[15] The modern world needs the fruitfulness that is derived from the scientific truth as well as the fulfillment that comes from religious truth. Fruitfulness without fulfillment is incomplete, and there can be no fulfillment without fruitfulness.

In the view of Einstein, religious truth is and remains relevant in the modern world in the midst of its scientific feats. Scientific truth and religious truth are complementary. As he expressed, the matter, "For science can only ascertain what is, but not what should be, and outside of its domain value judgments of all kinds remain necessary. Religion, on the other hand, deals only with evaluations of human thought and action: it cannot justifiably speak of facts and relationships between facts. According to this interpretation, the well-known conflicts between religion and science in the past must all be ascribed to a misapprehension. For example, a conflict arises when a religious community insists on the absolute truthfulness of all statements recorded in the Bible."[17] For religion to have a proper relevance, it must know its boundaries and maintain its domain. Likewise, science must respect religious boundaries.

From the Buddhist perspective on the relevance of religion in the modern world, the monk Mathieu Ricard in *The Quantum and the Lotus* said that there are some basic questions that are fundamental to the modern person which only religion, not science, can answer. Such questions concern our existence. Accordingly he wrote, "As for science's applications, they generally concern our health, life expectancy, freedom of action, and comfort . . . If we think about the moments that give most meaning to our lives, we generally mention love, friendship tenderness, joy, the beauty of a natural landscape, inner peace or altruism. Science that simply focuses on outer phenomena has very little to do with any of these."[18] But are all these necessary and relevant to modern society? Yes, they are, and their truths lie within the confines of religion. Hence, religion remains relevant to modernity.

Conclusion.

The secularism of the modern world gave birth to skepticism, which challenged the veracity of religious statements or religious truth. This in turn expressed itself in many other forms. As expressed by Haught, "In the modern intellectual world a good deal of skepticism about religion appeared. It has three distinct layers, though all three interpenetrate. We shall call them respectively rationalism, scientism and suspicion.[19]

Amidst all the anti-religious "isms" of modernity, has religion been extinct? No. Do people still look unto religion as a source of truth, and does religion satisfies human longing for truth in the modern world amidst scientific advancement? Yes. This goes to show that religion will continue to be relevant as a source of truth in the modern world.

However, there is need for caution both on the part of science and modernity, and religion. Religion should not claim to offer absolute truth on the questions of "how." Its view here should be an opinion that looks unto science for clarity. Science on the other hand should not claim to have absolute truth on questions of "why." It should look unto religion for clarity. As affirmed by Thiselton, "The contrast is a useful one because it begins to explain how TRUTH in the natural science and TRUTH in religion is often complementary, and need not to be competitive; yet at the same time they are not compartmentalized as they addressed different, self-contained segments of reality."[20]

Notes.

1. Karl Marx and Friedrich Engels, *On Religion*. (New York: Shoken Books, 1964), 41.
2. David W. Shenk, *Global Gods: Exploring the Role of Religion in Modern Societies*. (Waterloo: Herald Press, 1995), 325.
3. William L. Reese, *Dictionary of Philosophy and Religion*. (New York: Humanity Books, 1999), 783.
4. Shenk, *Global Gods*, 327.
5. Varadaraja V. Raman, "On Scientific and Religious Truths." http://www.metanexus.net/Magazine/ tabid/68 . . . (accessed November 6, 2007)
6. Ibid.
7. Elder, A. E., "Book Review" in *Jstor Website*, http://links. jstor.org/sici?sici=1752. (accessed November 6, 2007)
8. Gary E. Kessler, *Philosophy of Religion: Towards a Global Perspective* (New York: Wadsworth Publishing Company, 1999), 505-506.
9. Albert Einstein, "On Religion and Science," http://www. spaceandmotion.com/Theology-Albert-Einstein.htm (accessed November 6, 2007)
10. Ibid.
11. Mathieu Ricard and Trinh Xuan Thuan, *The Quantum and the Lotus*. (New York: Three River Press, 2001), 276.
12. Vatican II, *Gaudium et Spes: The Pastoral Constitution of the Church in the Modern World*, 1965, nos. 5-10
13. "Vatican wants to end battle with Science," MSNBC News November 3, 2005, http://www.msnbc.msn.com/ id/9913712/ (accessed November 6, 2007)
14. Albert Einstein, "Science and religion," http://www. sacred-text.com/aor/einstein/einsci.htm (accessed November 7, 2007)

15. Masao Abe, *Zen and Western Thought.* (Hawaii: University of Hawaii Press, 1985), 241.
16. Raman, "On scientific and Religious Truth," Ibid.
17. Einstein, "Science and Religion," Ibid.
18. Ricardo and Thuan, *The Quantum and the Lotus,* 268.
19. John F. Haught, *What is Religion.* (New York: Paulist Press, 1990), 212.
20. Anthony C. Thiselton, *A Concise Encyclopedia of the Philosophy of Religion.* (Michigan: Baker Academic, 2002), 279.

7.2LUDWIG FEUERBACH'S, FRIEDRICH NIETZSCHE'S, AND SIGMUND FREUD'S CRITIQUE OF RELIGION: THE STRENGTHS AND WEAKNESSES.

Introduction.

When it comes to the critique of religion and, perhaps, the origin of mordern atheism, certain names ring bell. Prominent among such names are Ludwig Feuerbach, Sigmund Freud, and Friedrich Nietzsche. These men, in their various ways denied God and religion any relevance in modern society. For Feuerbach, God was only a projection of the mind; he does not exit in reality. Freud on his part saw religion as nothing but an illusion, while Nietzsche pronounced God as dead with the Cathedral towers as his monument. Interestingly, apart from Frued, these men were Germans. According to Karl Marx, the German period of these men was a period marked by atheism. In his words, "For Germany the criticism of religion is in the main complete, and criticism of religion is the premise of all criticism." Expressing the same view as Marx, Karren Armstrong, went on to say:

> This was the century in which Ludwig Feuerbach, Karl Marx, Charles Darwin, Friedrich Nietzsche and Sigmund Freud forged philosophies and scientific interpretations of reality which had no place for God . . . a significant number of people were beginning to feel that if God was not yet dead, it was the duty of rational, emancipated human beings to kill him.[2]

The focus of this essay is on what Feuerbach, Nietzsche, and Freud saw in religion that made them criticize it at time when majority of the people saw religion as a source of succor.

Feuerbach's Critique of Religion.

Feuerbach's radical turning point against religion came from his studies of Hegel's interpretation of religion. According to Jones, he saw the passing away of religion as a key to the progress of scientific society.[3]

Central to Feuerbach's critique of religion is his understanding of God as a projection of the human mind. In his work, *The Essence of Christianity*, he wrote:

> The object of religion is a selected object; the most excellent, the first, the Supreme Being; it essentially presupposes a critical judgment, a discrimination between the divine and the non-divine, between that which is worthy of adoration and that which is not worthy. And here may be applied, without any limitation, the proposition: the object of any subject is nothing else than the subject's own nature taken objectively. Such as are a man's thought and dispositions, such is his God: so much worth as a man has, so much and no more has his God.[4]

This projection of God according to man's nature arose out of wants, needs, loneliness, comfort, security, and feeling of dependency. The divine being is nothing else other the human being, or, rather the human nature purified, freed from the limits of individual man, made objectified. He de-robed religion of divine origin or authority, and traces its origin to feeling and nature. He believed that the feeling of dependence in man is the source of religion; but the object of its dependence is nature. The assertion that religion is innate and natural to man is false. Religion is the manifestation of man's conception of himself.[5]

Nietzsche's Critique of Religion.

Central to his critique of religion is the idea that "God is dead." In his work *The Gay Science*[6], using the parable of a lunatic in search of God, Nietzsche wrote, "Do we hear nothing as yet of the noise of the gravediggers who are burying God? Do we smell nothing yet of the divine decomposition? Gods, too, decompose. God is dead.

God remains dead, and we have killed him. What after all are these churches now if they are not the tombs and sepulchers of God?"[7]

He accused religion of cruelty, and God in whose name this cruelty was done, must be sacrificed as a price. In *Beyond Good and Evil*, he said, there is a great ladder of religious cruelty, with many rounds; but three of these are most important. Once upon a time men sacrificed human beings to their God, and perhaps just those they loved the best. During the moral epoch of mankind, they sacrificed the strongest instinct they possessed, their "nature;" this festal joy shines in the cruel glances of ascetic and "anti-natural" fanatics. Finally, what remained to be sacrificed? Was it not necessary in the end for men to sacrifice God himself? To sacrifice God for nothingness – this paradoxical mystery of the ultimate cruelty has been reserved for the rising generation; we all know something of this already.[8]

Furthermore, he believed that religion perpetuates suffering and that there is nothing admirable in Christianity and Buddhism. He described these 'paramount' religions, as 'the religions of sufferers', and among the principal causes which have kept man upon a lower level, and had, in deed and in truth, worked for the deterioration of the European race.[9]

He described religion and its teachings as fictitious and lies, and tend towards "servile negation that diminishes humankind."[10]

Freud's Critique of Religion.

In Freud's view, religion emerged out of man's need for security and protection. He compared this need to that of a child relying first on the mother, and later on the father for his existence and survival. Applying this concept of child-mother-father relationship and dependency to the origin of religion, Freud said, when the growing individual find that he is destined to remain a child for ever, that he can never do without protection against strange superior powers, he lends those powers the features belonging to his father; he creates for himself the gods whom he dreads, whom he seeks to propitiate, and whom he nevertheless entrusts with his own protection. Thus his longing for a father is a motive identical with his need for protection against the consequences of his human weakness. The defense against childish helplessness is what lends its characteristics feature to the adult's reaction to the helplessness he has to acknowledge – a reaction which is precisely the formation of religion.[11] Continuing, he wrote in *Totem and Taboo*, "The psycho-analysis of individual human beings, . . . teaches us with quite special insistence that the god of each of them is formed in the likeness of his father, that his personal relation to God depends on his relation to his father in the flesh . . . and that at the bottom God is nothing other an exalted father"[12]

Freud reduced religion to the level of neurosis. Religious ideas are illusions, delusions, and unreal. He said,

> These (religious ideas) which are given out of teachings, are not precipitates of experiences or end-results of thinking: they are illusions, fulfillment of the oldest, strongest and most urgent wishes of mankind. The secret of their strength lies in the strength of those wishes . . . What is characteristic of illusion is that they are derived from human wishes. In this respect, they come near to psychiatric delusions. In the case of delusion, they contradict reality.[13]

The only road that leads to reality is not religion, but science, and the belief that there is a benevolent God, moral order, and after-life are all mere wishes and delusions.

The Strengths of These Critiques.

At a time when so many wrongs were being committed in the name of religion, these eminent scholars awakened the conscious of men to what should be the roles and limits of religion in the society. They challenged the intelligence of theologians who came up with better responses, to the advantage of religion, towards the functions of religion in a modern society.

In their critiques they tried to trace the origin of religion and God. Their short comings not withstanding in this regard, they contributed immensely to the development of the study of history or science of religion, or comparative religion.

Their aim was to liberate society from excessive religious dogmatism and to pave way for the emergence of science. According to Thiselton, they saw their critiques of religion as a philosophy of liberation, with social and political consequences for the future. The new gospel is true humanism: the love and unreduced dignity of humankind.[14] This, I may say, was a cause in the right direction.

The Weaknesses of These Critiques.

These scholars denied God of any ontological existence. Freud and Feuerbach reduced him to a mere wish and a projection of the human mind. Even in His existence as a wish and projection, God was declared DEAD by Nietzsche. These theories lack merit and truth. Commenting on this, Thiselton said, "It is not true that something cannot exist merely because we also wish and hope for it to exist. In actuality, the status of human wishes remains irrelevant to the ontological statue of God. Freud and Feuerbach would need to demonstrate that wishes or projections of God constitute the exclusive and exhaustive grounds for ascribing ontological reality to God, without remainder."[15]

They failed to realize that man, and not religion in itself was the problem. Again, religion does not only teach suffering, it also emphasizes happiness and comfort. It does not dehumanize man, but teaches and defends human dignity as evident in the social teachings of the Church through the centuries.

Finally, their critiques were mainly on theistic religions, especially Christianity. They failed to understand that not all religions are theistic. Religion is more than Christianity.

Conclusion.

Although these eminent scholars tend to do away with religion and God, they did not succeed. God and religion still flourish in the midst of heavy of criticisms. Nietzsche was right by saying that, 'all that exists consists of interpretation.' If this is so, Nietzsche concluded, 'we shall never be rid of God so long as we still believe in grammar.'[16]

Indeed, society can never be rid of religion and God.

NOTES.

1. Karl Marx and Friedrich Engels, *On Religion.* (New York: Schoken Books, 1964), 41

2. Karen Armstrong, *A History of God.* (New York: Ballantine Books, 1993), 349.

3. Kile Jones, "A Critique of Ludwig Feuerbach's Philosophy of Religion" in *Metareligion.* http://www.meta-religion.com/ Philosophy/Articles/Philosophy_of_religion/critique_of_ ludwig . (accessed August 29, 2007).

4. Ludwig Feuerbach, *The Essence of Christianity.* (New York: Harper & Row, Publishers, 1957), 12.

5. Feuerbach, *The Essence of Religion.* (New York: Prometheus Books, 2004), 1.

6. Friedrich Nietzsche, *The Gay Science.* (New York: Vintage, 1974), no. 124.

7. Nietzsche, *The Gay Science,* 125.

8. Friedrich Nietzsche, *Beyond Good and Evil.* (Kansas: Digireads. com Books, 2005), no. 55.

9. Ibid., no. 62

10. Anthony Thiselton, *A Concise Encyclopedia of the Philosophy of Religion.*

(Michigan: Baker Academic, 2002), 200.

11. Sigmund Freud, *The Future of Illusion.* (New York: W. W. Norton & Company, (1961), 24.

12. Sigmund Freud, *Totem and Taboo.* (New York: Norton & Company, 1950), 182.

13. Freud, *The Future of Illusion,* 30.

14. Anthony Thiselton, *A Concise Encyclopedia of the Philosophy of Religion.*

(Michigan: Baker Academic, 2002), 100.

15. Ibid.

16. Ibid., 200.

7.3 KARL MARX'S CRITIQUE OF RELIGION: STRENGTHS AND WEAKNESSES, AND ITS APPLICATION TO BUDDHISM.

Introduction.

Karl Marx (1818-1883) lived in a period of heavy critique of religion.[1] This was almost the same period of Ludwig Feuerbach (1804-1874), and Sigmund Freud (1856-1939). In this period, God who is the center of religion in the West, was seen as a mere projection and construction of human mind. There was nothing sacred about God and religion. To destroy or demolish the structure called religion was indeed a major and primary task for Karl Marx. But one may ask: Why was Marx so critical and negative about religion? To answer this question properly, I will begin with a brief background survey of Marx. Understanding his background will provide a good prologue to his critique of religion.

Karl Marx's Background.

Karl Heinrich Marx (1818-1883), a philosopher, social scientist, historian, and a revolutionary, was born in the German City of Trier into a Jewish family that later converted to Christianity for economic and political reasons. He attended the University of Bonn. In Bonn, "Marx became a member of the Young Hegelian Movement. This group, which involved the theologians Bruno Bauer and David Friedrich Strauss, produced a radical critique of Christianity, and by implication, the liberal opposition to the Prussian autocracy."[2] His membership of this movement shaped his radical and critical attitude towards religion in general and Christianity in particular. The Young Hegelians, consisted of a group of philosophers and journalists circling around Ludwig Feuerbach, made use of Hegel's dialectical method, separated from its theological content, as a powerful weapon for the critique of established religion and politics.[3]

It can be said that Karl Marx's mission was to emancipate, to liberate society and people from the grip and oppression of religion and politics. He later took an atheistic stand, seeing God, through the eyes of Feuerbach, as a projection.

Karl Marx's Critique of Religion.

Karl Marx's critique of religion derives mainly from his critique of Hegel's philosophy of right in 1844, and from his theses on Feuerbach written in 1845. He saw religion as nothing but the work and creation of man, as against the notion of religion as a divine institution. Being man-made, religion was for him like any other social institution that humanity created. He said,

> Man makes religion, religion does not make man. In other words, religion is the self-consciousness and self-feeling of man who has either not yet found himself or has already lost himself again. But man is no abstract being squatting outside the world. Man is in the world of man, the state and society. This state, this society, produces religion."[4]

Like every other societal realities, religion depends upon society; its material and economic realities. It is wholly dependent upon the productive force of the society. Marx wrote,

> The religious world is but the reflex of the real world. And for a society based upon the production of commodities, in which the producers in general enter into social relations with one another by treating their products as commodities and values, whereby they reduced their individual private labor to the standard of homogeneous human labor – for such a society Christianity with its *cultus* of abstract man, especially in its bourgeois developments, Protestantism, Deism, & co., is the most fitting form of religion."[5]

For Marx, therefore, religion is empty of anything sacred or divine. It is purely the work of man. Commenting in this, Cline said that for Marx, religion can only be understood in relation to other social systems and the economic structures of society. In fact, religion is only dependent upon economics, so much so that the actual religious doctrines are almost irrelevant.[6]

Karl Marx equally understood religion as an instrument of oppression used, by the ruling to oppress the proletariat. This formed his bitterness or critique of religion, especially, Christianity. He wrote in his paper entitled *The Communism of the Paper Rheinischer Beobachter*, of September 12, 1847,

> The social principles of Christianity justified the slavery of Antiquity, glorified the serfdom of the Middle Ages and equally know, when necessary, how to defend the oppression of the proletariat, although they make a pitiful face over it. The social principle of Christianity preach the necessity of a ruling and an oppressed class, and all they have for the latter is the pious wish the former will be charitable. They transfer the consistorial councilors' adjustment of all infamies to heaven and thus justify the further existence of those infamies on earth. They declare all vile acts of oppressors against the oppressed to be either the just punishment of original sin and other sins or trials the Lord in his infinite wisdom imposes on those redeemed. The social principles of Christianity preach cowardice, self-contentment, abasement, submission, and dejection.[7]

From the above understanding of religion, Karl Marx drew his conclusion that religion is the source of all distress. He said, "Religious distress is at the same time the expression of real distress and the protest against real distress. Religion is the sigh of the oppressed creature, the heart of a heartless world, just as it is the spirit of spiritless situation. It is the opium of the people."[8] In essence, Marx is saying that religion is an instrument to pacify the masses, to offer them assurance of an unrealizable happiness, which he called illusory happiness, to offer false hope to the hopeless, to pretend to heal the wound of the injured, while in fact it (religion) is part of the injury. As a result, he said, "the criticism of religion is therefore in criticism of the vale of woes, the halo of which is religion."[9]

Marx believed that "the abolition of religion as the illusory happiness of the people is required for their real happiness. The demand to give up the illusions about its condition is the demand to give up a condition, which needs illusion. Religion is the only illusory sun which revolves around man as long man does revolve around himself."[10]

Again, Marx heavily criticized religion because it undermines the true dignity of man, denies him freedom, and enslaves him. It pretends to offer man freedom, but the reverse is the case. To liberate man from the shackles of religion was for him a task to be accomplished by destroying religion. Accordingly he declared,

The criticism of religion ends with the teaching that man is the highest essence for man, hence with the categorical imperative to overthrow all relations, in which man is debased, enslaved, abandoned, despicable essence; relations which can be better describe by the cry of a Frenchman when it was planned to introduce a tax on dogs: poor dog! They want to treat you as a human being!" [11]

Religion is one such relation that must be overthrown if man is to regain his dignity.

Furthermore, Marx saw religion as hypocritical. It teaches one, it does another thing. Hear him,

> Has not Christianity declaimed against private property, against marriage, against the State? Has it not preached in place of these, charity and poverty, celibacy and mortification of the flesh, monastic life and Mother church? Christian Socialism is but the holy water with which the priest consecrates the heart-burnings of the aristocrats. [12]

Analyzing Marx's concept of religion, Cline observed that Marx has three reasons for disliking religion.

> First, it [religion] is irrational. Second, it negates all that dignifies man. Third, religion is hypocritical. Although it might profess valuable principles, it sides with the oppressors. Jesus advocated helping the poor, but the Christian church merged with the oppressive Roman State, taking part in the enslavement of people for centuries. In the Middle Ages, the Catholic Church preached about heaven, but acquired as much property and power as possible. Martin Luther preached the ability of each individual to interpret the Bible, but sided with aristocratic rulers and against peasants who fought economic and social oppression.[13]

Discussing Martin Luther and religion, Karl Marx said, Luther overcame bondage out of devotion by replacing it by bondage out of conviction. He freed the body of chain because he enchained the heart.[14] Religion claims to offer a solution to a problem buts end up creating more problems than it hypocritically pretends to solve.

Regarding his attitude towards God, Marx shared the view of Feuerbach, that God is a human Projection. In his view, man creates religion, not just religion, but all that is sacred in religion as a tool of enslavement. As Thiselton puts it, "Marx proposes, rather that projected beliefs about God come to be utilized by a ruling or 'established' class to promote submissive contentment, or at least acquiescence, or the part of the oppressed masses."[15] Similarly, if religion, which projected God, is an illusion, it goes to say that God, the product and center of religion, is also an illusion. As a matter of fact Marx declared his stand in his critique as one who is against religion and against God. According to Cline, in the preface of his doctoral dissertation, Marx adopted as his motto the word of the Greek hero Prometheus who defied the gods to bring fire to humanity: 'I hate all gods.'[16]

Marx's most practical objection to religion, says Thiselton, was that by illusory promise of 'reward' for acquiescence and obedience, institutional faith blocked the way to action on the part of the masses towards their liberation from oppression by social, political, and violent revolution. Religion encouraged respect for the 'order' of the established powers, disguising their role as oppressors.[17]

It was because of such 'negative' roles of religion that Karl Marx vehemently criticized religion and wished that it be done away with.

The Strength of Karl Marx's Critique of Religion.

Karl Marx gave a very useful insight into the relationship of religion and society.

Truly, religion cannot be understood independently of society. He rightly observed that those in power used religion as instrument of oppression, and religion willingly played the role. Hence Marx's famous statement that 'religion is the opium of the people.' What Marx's said so many years ago remains true of religion today, especially in most of the developing countries of Africa where I come from. Many people are exploited there in the name of religion. The poor are pacified with such biblical passages like "Blessed are the poor: there is the kingdom of heaven. Blessed are you who hunger now: you shall be satisfied. Blessed are you who weep now: you shall laugh. Blessed are you when people hate you . . . Rejoice and be glad, for your reward will be great in heaven. "[18] In this type of situation the rich and the Church get richer while the poor get poorer hoping to get their own share of happiness in heaven as religion promise them. That was the reason why Marx described religion as the sigh of oppressed creatures, and the abolition of religion as the illusory happiness of the people is required for their real happiness.

Again, the strength of Marx's critique of religion also lies in his view that religion is hypocritical. According to Marx, Christianity declaimed against private property, against the State, preached poverty, celibacy and mortification of the flesh. On the contrary, the Church owned all the biggest estates, the Church had alliance with the State in oppressing the poor , the Church even exercised political power more than the State (e.g. the Vatican City State or Papal State), the Church preached poverty but was herself very rich. She preached celibacy, but the priests were living in clerical immorality. I wonder what Marx would say if he were to witness the clergy sexual abuse scandal that happened in America. Simply put, much of what Marx said about religion and hypocrisy is still true of religion today. For example, Islam is said to be a religion of peace, but in the name of Islam, the worst form of violence is being committed globally.

The Weakness of Marx's Critiques of Religion.

As Cline would say, as interesting and insightful as Marx's critiques of religion are, they are without their problems.[19]

First, Marx's reduced religion to a single system that is Christianity. In as much his critiques can and do by extension touch other religion, his critique was essentially critique of Christianity rather than a critique of religion. In other words he has a limited insight of what religion is.

His reduction of religion to only a social system, and a product of economic and material realities do not hold much ground. Religion may be a social institution, but it goes beyond that as practical experiences have proved. There are divine elements in religion.

Again, by saying that religion is the 'heart of heartless society, and the spirit of a spiritless world', Marx indirectly acknowledged that religion is not all that bad. At least, it is the consciences, the heart and the spirit of a world 'without conscience, heart and soul'. It gives people the reason to hold on to life and to continue living.

Applying Marx's Critique of Religion to Buddhism.

In applying Marx's critique of religion to Buddhism, two statements readily come to my mind: Either Marx was completely ignorant of Buddhism or he was aware of it but did not consider it (Buddhism) as a religion.

Although, Marx's critique religion is more a critique of Christianity, it can, by extension, be applied to Buddhism. Marx reduction of religion to a product of society and the creation of man apply equally to Buddhism. This is because Buddhism as religion came out of society and is sustained within the society. Also, it was made by man, the Buddha. As Marx would say, 'man, makes religion, religion does not make man.' That is to say, Siddhartha Gautama (who later became the Buddha) made Buddhism, Buddhism did not make Siddhartha. If religion is bad because of this, then Marx would also say that Buddhism, as a religion, is bad. Looking at it from another angle, Marx's critique of religion would exempt Buddhism. One of the reasons why Marx criticized religion was because it used the concept of heaven to make people perpetually poor by assuring them of a better place and happiness in the heaven, and by teaching them that their oppression and suffering were trials which God in his infinite wisdom gives them. Buddhism as religion has no heaven and does not preach the concept happiness in the other world. It has no God and so does not see suffering as a trial from a 'loving' God to his people. You suffer because of your own bad karma. Not because of original sin, or from God. You achieve your own liberation through your own effort. Karl Marx would probably have applauded Buddhism. However, he would also criticize Buddhism on this as well. Buddhism says suffering is in the mind, Marx says that it arises from an unjust economic system. For Marx, Buddhism prevents economic change because it says it is all in the mind. Thus, Buddhism protects the oppressor, Marx would conclude.

Conclusion.

As Helmut Gollwitzer observes, "Marxist criticisms of religion may well apply to certain examples of the phenomenon of religion in the empirical life of faith communities or churches. However, on what grounds can this critique be applied as a universal explanation of all religion at all times."[20] As a philosopher, social scientist, historian, and a revolutionary, Marx did his best in his analysis and understanding of religion. I give him credit. He was a brilliant scholar, but his critique of religion was too narrow, and limited the western concept of religion especially Christianity. His critique cannot stand the test when placed side by side with all the religions of the world.

Notes

1. Karl Marx and Friedrich Engels, *On Religion* (New York: Schoken Books, 1964), 41

2. The History Guide Website. "Lectures on Modern European Intellectual History." http://www.historyguide.org/intellect/marx.html (accessed September 5, 2007)

3. "Karl Marx", http://en.wikipedia.org/wiki/karl_marx (accessed September 5, 2007).

4. Marx and Engels, *On Religion*, 41.

5. Ibid., 135.

6. Austin Cline, "*Karl Marx's Analysis of Religion*" in *About. com: Agnosticism/Atheism.* http://atheism.about.com/od/philosophyofreligion/a/marx_4.htm?p=1 (accessed August 29, 2007)

7. Marx and Engels, *On Religion*, 82-83.

8. Ibid., 42

9. Ibid.

10. Ibid.

11. Ibid., 50.

12. Ibid., 89.

13. Cline, Ibid.

14. Marx and Engels, Ibid, 89.

15. Anthony Thiselton, *A Concise Encyclopedia of the Philosophy of Religion.*

(Michigan: Baker Academic, 2002), 178.

16. Cline, Ibid.

17. Thiselton, *Encyclopedia of the Philosophy of Religion*, 180

18. Luke 6:20-23.

19. Cline, Ibid.

20. Helmut Gollwitzer, *The Christian Faith and the Marxist Criticism of Religion.* (Edinburgh: St. Andrew, 1970), 28.

7.4 A CRITICAL ANALYSIS OF FREUD'S AND ELIADE'S VIEWS OF THE RELATIONSHIP BETWEEN RELIGION AND REALITY.

Introduction.

Sigmund Freud and Mircea Eliade are like two polar opposites in matters of religion. Freud was a psychologist, and anti-religion. On the other hand, Eliade was a professor of religion with a soft spot for religion. What we are about to discuss in this paper are divergent and opposite views of the relationship between religion and reality.

To do justice to the topic, I will first present the views of both scholars on the relationship between religion and reality. This will provide a deeper insight into a critical analysis of their views on the subject under discussion.

Freud's View of the Relationship between Religion and Reality.

Freud understands of the relationship of religion and reality was conditioned by his understanding of religion, its origin, and its role in life. His knowledge of psychoanalysis heavily influenced his view of his views on religion.

In Freud's view, religion emerged out of man's need for security and protection. He compared this need to that of a child relying first on the mother, and later on the father for his existence and survival. Freud wrote, "The mother who satisfies the child's hunger becomes its first lover-object and certainly its first protection against all the undefined dangers which threatens it in the external world . . . the mother is soon replaced by the stronger father, who retains that position for the rest of childhood."[1] Applying this concept of child-mother-father relationship and dependency to the origin of religion, Freud further said, when the growing individual finds that he is destined to remain a child forever, that he can never do without protection against strange superior powers, he lends those powers the features belonging to his father; he creates for himself the gods whom he dreads, whom he seeks to propitiate, and whom he nevertheless entrusts with his own protection. Thus, his longing for a father is a motive identical with his need for protection against the consequences of his human weakness. The defense against childish helpless is what lends its characteristics feature to the adult's reaction to the helplessness he has to acknowledge – *a reaction which is precisely the formation of religion.*[2] (Italics is mine for emphasis)

It is obvious from the above citation that Freud saw God as a projection based on the understanding of his father. On this, Freud in *Totem and Taboo* said,

> The psycho-analysis of individual human beings, . . . teaches us with quite special insistence that the god of each of them is formed in the likeness of his father, that his personal relation to God depends on his relation to his father in the flesh . . . and that at the bottom God is nothing other an exalted father.[3]

According to Thiselton, Freud's understanding of religion and God derives heavily on developmental and evolutional theories of the human race and of the individual. Religion is, therefore, associated with the infantile stage of human person, and also the stage of totem and taboo in the evolution of the human race.[4] In Freud's view, there is no reality out there that is called God. It is only a concept of mind, formed and projected by man. He believed that it is natural to man to personify everything he wants to understand in other later to control it, and religious ideas have arisen from the same need, as have all the other achievements of civilization.[5]

He believed that religion could not lead to reality. Religious ideas are mere beliefs and claims that are unverifiable. They are 'truths" meant to be believed because the ancestors believed in them and handed them down to us and they are unquestionable. In fact, religious ideas, according to Freud are full of contradictions revisions, falsifications, and where they speak of factual confirmations, they are themselves unconfirmed.[6] Freud reduced religion to the level of neurosis. Religion is an illusion; its ideas are delusions, and unreal. He said,

> These (religious ideas) which are given out of teachings,
> are not precipitates of experiences or end-results of
> thinking: they are illusions, fulfillment of the oldest,
> strongest and most urgent wishes of mankind. The secret
> of their strength lies in the strength of those wishes . . .
> What is characteristic of illusion is that they are derived
> from human wishes. In this respect, they come near
> to psychiatric delusions. In the case of delusion, they
> contradict reality."[7]

The only road that leads to reality is not religion, but science, and the belief that there is a benevolent God, moral order, and after-life are all mere wishes and delusions. Freud best describes what may appear to the religious man as reality as projections of inward perceptions towards something he feels to be external. He said, "The projection outward of internal perceptions is a primitive mechanism, to which, for instance, our sense perceptions are subject, and which therefore normally plays a large parting determining the form taken by our external world."[8]

In sum, in Freud's view, religion cannot lead to reality. What appear to be true connections between religion and reality is nothing but a delusion according to Sigmund Freud.

Eliade's View of the Relationship between Religion and Reality.

For Eliade, religion has an intrinsic and inseparable relationship with reality.

Religion and reality are interwoven. Religion gives meaning to reality, and helps man to understand reality. The basis of religion for Eliade is the hierophany. The term "hierophany", (from the Greek roots *hieros* – "sacred", "holy"—, and *epiphaneia* – appearance) signifies a manifestation of the Sacred. It occurs frequently in the works of the religious historian Mircea Eliade as an alternative to a more restrictive term *theophany.*"[9] Hierophany divides the sacred from the profane, and is the basis of all realities. Eliade maintains that,

> It could be said the history of religions – from the most
> primitive to the most highly developed – is constituted
> by a great number of hierophanies, by manifestations of
> sacred realities . . . When the sacred manifests itself in any
> hierophany, there is not only a break in the homogeneity
> of space; there is also revelation of an absolute reality, . . .
> The manifestation of he sacred ontologically founds the
> world. [10]

As the real, the sacred gives meaning to existence, and to live is to be in constant touch with sacred. As Eliade put it, the sacred reveals Absolute Reality and at same time makes orientation possible; hence it founds the world in the sense that it fixes the limits and establishes the order of the world. It is the source of life and fecundity.[11] Religious man's desire to live in the sacred is in fact equivalent to his desire to take up his abode in objective reality. For the primitives as for the man of all pre-modern societies, the sacred is equivalent to *power*, it is saturated with *being*. Sacred power means reality and at the same time enduringness and efficacy. Thus, it is easy to understand that the religious man deeply desires *to be,* to participate in *reality,* to be saturated with power. Religious reality for Eliade is real and absolute. It is not an inward projection, as Freud termed it. It transcends it world and gives the world its essence. Accordingly, Eliade said that the absolute reality, *the sacred*, transcends this world but manifests itself in this world, thereby sanctifying it and making it real.[12]

In sum, Eliade maintained that there is no separation between religion and reality. It is in the religious life that one experiences, relates with, and participates in the really real.

Conclusion.

Having analyzed Freud and Eliade's view of the relationships between religion and reality, I quickly want to point that both scholars went to negatives extremes. Freud denied religion of any concrete relation to reality, which, in fact, is a wrong view. Experience has shown that they are truths and realities outside the realm of science and psychology. Freud has a limited understanding of religion. According to Thiselton, Freud does not carefully compare alternative models of the nature of religion. His views remain selective and speculative.[13] Religion goes beyond a quest for the satisfaction of personal need. In the words of Webster, Freud's original theoretical system, his habits of thought and his entire attitude to scientific research are so far removed from any responsible method of enquiry that no intellectual approach basing itself upon these is likely to endure.[14]

For Eliade to describe religion as the only basis of reality is unrealistic. There are truths or realities outside the scope of religion. It is evident that some religious beliefs initially taken to be the absolute truth and reality have been proven wrong by modern science. In as much as I agree with Eliade that there is a real relationship between religion and reality, I wish to say that there are scientific realities beyond religion, as there are religious realities beyond science.

Notes.

1. Sigmund Freud, *The Future of Illusion*. (New York: W. W. Norton & Company, (1961), 24.

2. Ibid.

3. Sigmund Freud, *Totem and Taboo* (New York: Norton & Company, 1950), 182.

4. Thiselton, *A Concise Encyclopedia of the Philosophy of Religion*. (Michigan: Baker Academic, 2002), 111.

5. Freud, *The Future of Illusion*, 21.

6. Ibid., 27.

7. Ibid., 30.

8. Freud, *Totem and Taboo*, 81.

9. "Hierophany",http://en.wikipedia.org/wiki/Hierophany (accessed September 10, 2007).

10. Mircea Eliade, *The Sacred and the Profane: The Nature of Religion*. (New York: Harcourt, Inc. 1987), 11, 21.

11. Ibid., 30.

12. Ibid., 202.

13. Thiselton, Ibid., 112.

14. Richard Webster, "Critique of Sigmund Freud" http://en.wikipedia.org/wiki/sigmundfreud#critical_reaction (accessed September 10, 2007).

7.5 "BEYOND THE TEXT": A HERMENEUTICAL INTERPRETATION OF THE VIMALAKIRTI SUTRA, "THE DHARMA IS NOT A SECURE REFUGE", IN THE LIGHT OF ETIENNE LAMOTTE'S ESSAY: "THE ASSESSMENT OF TEXTUAL INTERPRETATION IN BUDDHISM."

Introduction.

One of the major problems that every established religion faces after the demise of its founder or immediate disciples, is the problem of accessing and understanding the mind and intention of the founder as contained in his sayings and teaching (oral and or written). An attempt to get into the mind of the founder is what has given birth to what is today called *hermeneutics*, which is an art or science of interpretation, aimed towards a better understanding of what was said and has been written either directly by the founder himself or by later generations. This problem is not only peculiar to Buddhism, but extends to Judeo-Christian religions as well as Islam, and every other religion. As noted by Lopez, "The interpretation of sacred scripture is, of course, a concern which is not confined to the Judeo-Christian tradition. It is also a major issue in Buddhism . . . [that] has a vast sacred canon, a fact due both to the length of the Buddha's teaching career and to the posthumous attribution of many discourses to him, especially by the Mahayana."[1]

In this essay, we shall analyze the hermeneutical principles outlined by Lamotte as a tool to interpreting Buddhist texts. We shall use these principles to interpret the text "The Dharma is not a sure refuge."[2] A text taking from the Mahayana scripture, *The Vimalakirti Sutra.*

In this essay, we shall draw from the hermeneutical principles of Origen, Ricoeur, and other Buddhists scholars to illustrate our points.

The Hermeneutical Principles for Textual Interpretation in Buddhism in Lamotte's Essay.

Drawing from authoritative sources, especially, the *Mahapadesa*, Lamotte opined that the interpretation of Buddhist texts followed an agreeable format by Buddhist scholars. Chiefly among them is that the text must have some affinity with the Buddha's word, either by utterance or by attribution. For a text to be taken as the word of the Buddha certain criteria must be met. Accordingly,

> For a text to be considered as the word of the Buddha, it must be based on the authority of the Buddha himself, of a formally constituted community, of one of the several particularly learned 'elders'; it should further be in harmony with the doctrinal texts (sutras), the disciplinary collections (vinaya), and spirit of Buddhist philosophy.[3]

With the establishment of the authenticity regarding the sutra or the word as coming from the Buddha or at least in accordance to the teaching of the Buddha, the next task is "to supply a correct interpretation of it, to understand what the author is saying and, especially, what he is trying to say."[4] To achieve this interpretation and understating where does one look to? In addition to looking at the text and reading it as it is, one must also look beyond the text. Looking beyond the text here implies looking at the context, the audience, the background, and the spirit of the text. The reason to look beyond is that some religious texts are metaphorical and/or ambiguous. The meaning of the text may not be seen in face value or literal reading of text. This is exactly what Nagarjuna meant in this statement about the nature of the dharma,

> The dharma of the Buddha is immense, like the ocean. Depending on the aptitude of beings, it is expounded in various ways: sometimes it speaks of existence and sometimes of nonexistence, eternity or permanence, suffering or happiness, the self or the not-self; sometimes

it teaches the diligent practice of the threefold activity [of body, speech and mind] which include all good dharmas, and sometimes it teaches that all dharmas are intrinsically inactive . . . [5]

Applying this method of looking beyond the text to the textual interpretation of Buddhist text, Lamotte said:

The *Catuhpratisaranasutra* posits, under the name of refuge *(pratisarana)*, four rules of textual interpretation: (1) the doctrine *(dharma)* is the refuge and not the person *(purusa)*; (2) the spirit *(artha)* is the refuge and not the letter *(vyanaja)*; (3) the sutra of precise meaning *(nitartha)* is the refuge and not the sutra of provisional meaning *(neyartha)* ; (4) (direct) knowledge *(jnana)* is the refuge and not (discursive) consciousness *(vijnana)*.[6]

These four principles enunciated above by Lamotte are applicable to interpreting Buddhist texts of all traditions: Theravada, Mahayana, and Vajrayana.

In this paper, we shall apply the first two principles in interpreting a text, *"The dharma is not a secure refuge,"* from the Mahayana sutra, *The Holy Teaching of Vimalakirti.*

Application of Lamotte's Principles in Interpreting the Vimalakirti Sutra, *"The Dharma Is Not A Secure Refuge."*

The above text under consideration is derived from the discussion between Vimalakirti and Venerable Sariputra. Upon entering the house of Vimalakirti, Sariputra contemplated of the absence of a chair in the house. To this Vimalakirti asked him whether he was interested in the Dharma or in a chair. On declaring his intention in favor of the Dharma, Vimalakirti went ahead to expound the nature of the Dharma to the venerable. It was within this teaching that Vimalakirti uttered the sutra, "The Dharma is without acceptance or rejection. He who holds on to things or lets go of things is not interested in the Dharma but is interested in holding and letting go.

The Dharma is not a sure refuge. He who enjoys a secure refuge is not interested in the Dharma but is interested in a secure refuge." (Italics is mine).

Taking refuge in the Dharma is one of the three jewels in Buddhism[8] and this is very important in all Buddhist traditions. This refuge in the Dharma, as in the Buddha and the Sangha, is believed to be a secure refuge and not an illusive refuge. Again, because the Dharma is secure and firm, it is supposed to be the guide and teacher of the Sangha and all Buddhists after the entrance into the path of Nirvana by the Buddha. The Buddha himself did say, "After my death, the Dharma shall be your teacher. Follow the Dharma and you will be true to me."[9] The first principle of interpreting Buddhist textual texts in Lamotte essay is also an affirmation that the Dharma is the refuge.

From the above explanation that the Dharma is the guide and sure refuge for Buddhists, the sutra from Vimalakirti that the Dharma is not a secure refuge sounds either contradictory or undermining to the central Buddhists belief. However, is it truly contradictory or undermining? This hermeneutical question does not require a yes or no answer but rather requires explanation and interpretation to get the correct meaning of the sutra.

The first hermeneutical principle to apply in interpreting and understanding the text is to read or look not just in between the lines of text, but most importantly beyond the text. To express this using Lamotte's principle in his essay *Textual Interpretation in Buddhism,* the meaning and proper interpretation or understanding of the text is not in letter but in the spirit of the text. The question that one would ask is: what is Vimalakirti intending to say or to teach, by the statement 'The Dharma is without acceptance or rejection. He who holds on to things or let go of things is not interested in the Dharma but is interested in holding and letting go. The Dharma is not a sure refuge. He who enjoys a secure refuge is not interested in the Dharma but is interested in a secure refuge'? The *letter* implies that the Dharma is misleading, which of course is a wrong interpretation. The *spirit* is to proclaim and to teach the impermanence and emptiness of all things, including the Dharma and refuge in it.

205

This is the correct interpretation of the text, and it is in line with the basic Mahayana doctrine. This principle of looking beyond the text or the spirit rather than just the letter, calls the mind what Paul Ricoeur said regarding a discourse. According to Ricoeur, " . . . all discourse is produced as an event; as such, it is the counterpart of language understood as code or system . . . All discourse, we shall say, is realized as event but understood as meaning."[10] The connection between event and meaning as contained in a discourse brings about another polarity namely: sense and reference. What do we mean by sense and reference as it applies to discourse? It simply means, "Distinguishing between what is said by the sentence as a whole and by the words which compose it on the other hand, and that about which something is said on the other hand. To speak is to say something about something."[11] Applying this to our text, in this sutra, Vimalakirti used the insecurity of Dharma as a refuge to say something about something, i.e., the emptiness of all things, and not to say that the Dharma is deceptive or illusive.

Looking at Lamotte's principle of the real meaning of a text lying in the spirit and not in the letters, reminds me of the principle of textual interpretation of the Bible by the early fathers of the Church. It is stated that:

> Philo, a Jewish philosopher and contemporary of Jesus, employed platonic and stoic categories to interpret the Jewish scriptures. His general practices were adopted by the Christian Clement of Alexandria, who sought the allegorical sense of biblical texts . . . His successor Origen systematized these hermeneutical principles. Origen distinguished the literal, moral and spiritual senses but acknowledged the spiritual (i.e., allegorical) to be the highest. In the Middle Ages, Origen's threefold sense of scripture was expanded into a fourfold sense by a subdivision of the spiritual sense into the allegorical and the analogical (mystical interpretation).[12]

Furthermore, responding to those who adopted the literary interpretation of the Scriptures over and above the allegorical or spiritual sense, "Origen reasoned in the 4th book of his treatise On First Principles that, if the Bible is inspired by God, then it cannot be irrelevant, unworthy of God, or simply crude. If it ever appears to be in error then we have obviously missed its deeper meaning.[13] Again, Origen wrote that the "literalists of his day that they attack allegorical interpretation and want to teach that divine Scripture has nothing deeper than the text allows. Literalists [he complained], believe such things about [God] as would not be believed of the most savage and unjust of men. These 'Literalists' misunderstood the meaning of poetry, metaphors, parables and figures of speech and had no concept of the need to understand what the original author of the text was seeking to express to his audience."[14]

We can, by analogy, apply the allegorical interpretation to the text from the Vimalakirti sutra, to understand a spiritual teaching concerning the Dharma and not a literary teaching. Even when the Buddha said, let the Dharma be your teacher, I do not think that he meant it literarily. The statement has an allegorical meaning of placing the spirit of the text above the letter, as Lamotte would say "The spirit (artha) is the refuge and not the letter (vyanjana)."[15]

Conclusion.

From our discussion so far, it is clear that the proper interpretation and understanding of any Buddhist text or sutra takes more than the literary reading of the text. One has to consider the basic hermeneutical principle of text and context. Looking not just at the text but also the context, under which what was said was said, and the audience and the state of mind that the speaker was, and also who translated the text and from what language to what language, are very important. This will definitely take the hermeneutist or whoever is trying to interpret the text beyond the text itself. In going beyond the text, the *spirit* of the text takes precedence over the letter. This is what St. Paul meant when he said, "The written letters of the Law brings death, but the spirit gives life."[16]

Notes.

1. Donald S. Lopez, Jr. Ed., *Buddhist Hermeneutics.* (Delhi: Motilal Banarsidass Publishers, 1993), 1-2.
2. Robert A. F. Thurman, Trans., *The Holy Teaching of Vimalakirti.* (Pennsylvania: Pennsylvania State Univ. Press, 1976), 51.
3. Lopez, *Buddhist Hermeneutics*, 11.
4. Ibid.
5. Nagarjuna, *Le Traite de la Grande Vertu de Sagesse, vol. 2* (Louvain, 1949), 1074.
6. Lopez, *Buddhist Hermeneutics*, 12.
7. Thurman, *The Holy Teaching of Vimalakirti*, 50-51.
8. Mark Water, *Encyclopedia of World Religions, Cults and the Occult.* (Tennessee: A M G Publishers, 2006), 213.
9. Bukkyo Dendo Kyokai, *The Teaching of the Buddha.* (Tokyo: Kosaido Printing Co., Ltd, 1966), 15.
10. Paul Ricoeur, *Hermeneutics and the Human Sciences.* (New York: Cambridge Univ. Press, 1981), 167.
11. Ibid.
12. "Hermeneutics." *Encyclopedia Britannica Online*, http://www.search.eb.com/eb/article.9040159 (accessed March 4, 2008).
13. Joseph W. Trigg, *Origen.* (London: SCM Press, 1983), 120.
14. Andre Thevet, *Origin of Alexandria* (c.185 – c.254), http://www.earlychurch.org.uk/origen.php (accessed March 4, 2008).
15. Lopez, *Buddhist Hermeneutics*, 13.
16. 2 Cor. 3: 6

7.6 THE QUEST FOR TRUTH: A HERMENEUTICAL INTERPRETATION OF THE HEART SUTRA, "FORM IS EMPTINESS, EMPTINESS IS FORM", IN THE LIGHT OF THOMAS P. KASULIS' ESSAY: "TRUTH WORDS: THE BASIS OF KUKAI'S THEORY OF INTERPRETATION."

Introduction.

The issue of accessing, interpreting and understanding the meaning of given text as it occurred in a given sutra is one of the dominant issues that confronted and is still confronting every school of thought in Buddhism. This problem is not only peculiar to Buddhism, but extends to Judeo-Christian religion as well as Islam. As noted by Lopez, "The interpretation of sacred scripture is, of course, a concern which is not confined to the Judeo-Christian tradition. It is also a major issue in Buddhism . . . [that] has a vast sacred canon, a fact due both to the length of the Buddha's teaching career and to the posthumous attribution of many discourses to him, especially by the Mahayana."[1]

Different schools and scholars have approached this issue of interpretation differently. Some emphasize a literal interpretation, others adopt a symbolic method, and others still adopt textual analytical and analogical methods. Others, again, look for the meaning text beyond the text itself. There are those who propose a multiple method. For example:

> Philo, a Jewish philosopher and contemporary of Jesus, employed platonic and stoic categories to interpret the Jewish scriptures. His general practices were adopted by the Christian Clement of Alexandria, who sought the allegorical sense of biblical texts . . . His successor Origen systematized these hermeneutical principles. Origen distinguished the literal, moral and spiritual senses but acknowledged the spiritual (i.e., allegorical) to be the highest. In the Middle Ages, Origen's threefold sense of scripture was expanded into a fourfold sense by

a subdivision of the spiritual sense into the allegorical and the analogical (mystical interpretation).[2]

In this essay under consideration, the emphasis is on the quest of truth. In other words, where lies the truth content of a given text and how do we find it? In addressing this question, Thomas P. Kasulis, employed and analyzed the hermeneutical theory of Kukai, the founder of Shingon Japanese school of Buddhism. In this essay, we shall apply Kukai's principle in the interpreting and understanding the text from the Heart Sutra, "Form is emptiness, emptiness is form."[3]

A Brief Background Analysis.

This essay by Thomas P. Kasulis is based on the hermeneutical theory of Shingon Buddhism, which is one of the Japanese Buddhist schools or sects. This school draws its teaching from its founder, Kukai, "the eighth patriarch of esoteric Buddhism. Historically, *shingon* serves as one of the Sino-Japanese rendering for *mantra* or sacred incantation. Hence, the term itself suggests ritualistic practice. Ideologically, the two characters of *shingon* actually mean "truth word."[4] Hence, the title of this essay by Kasulis, is derived from the name of this school of Japanese Buddhism.

One of the sutras that has a very great influence on Kukai outside the Mahavairocana Sutra, is the Heart Sutra, a sutra on which Kukai wrote what scholars considers as his major work. This sutra (Heart Sutra) is very popular in Japan. It is on record that, "Today the Heart Sutra (Japan: Hannayashingyo) is still used in many schools of Japanese Buddhism, and over the centuries many commentaries have been composed on this sutra, the most popular of which is Kukai's *The Secret Key to the Heart Sutra* (Han-nya-shin-gyo-hiken). This particular commentary, by the fact that it is written from the standpoint of the Shingo School of Esoteric Buddhism, asserting that the Heart Sutra be in fact an esoteric text."[5] In this commentary, Kukai divided the Heart Sutra into five and gave an interpretation on each of them. Most of the hermeneutical principles he employed in his commentary are what Kasulis presented in this essay.

In this commentary, Kukai sought to present the hermeneutical principle to be applied in interpreting and understanding the 'truth words' in a given text or sutra. This connection and interest that Kukai had with the Heart Sutra influenced my choice of text from the Heart Sutra in discussing Thomas P. Kasulis' essay on Kukai's theory of interpretation in Japanese Buddhism.

The Hermeneutical Principles Contained In Kasulis' Essay.

A proper reading of this essay reveals multiple hermeneutical principles in the view of Shingon Japanese Buddhism, which one must apply in other to get the "truth words" of a particular text. These principles are:

i.) The true meaning of a text is not in the literary reading or understanding of the text. This first principle affirms that the meaning of text lies beyond the text itself. Expressing the hermeneutical view of Kukai, Kasulis writes, " . . . the text's true meaning is not in the letters written on the pages, but in the dynamics between the words and the reader."[6] This dynamic that happens between the words or text and reader is what Kukai called in esoteric language, *Dainichi*. Hence following this principle, Kukai, in his theory of interpretation believed that "every text, indeed everything whatsoever, is a symbolic expression of *Dainichi*, every text must have an esoteric dimension. Thus . . . the reader should be aware of the wondrous presence of the text itself; its verbal content (mind), its sound (intonation), and its very tangibility (body) are all manifestations of the *Dainichi* enlightenment. In other word, the dharmakaya expounds the dharma through every dharma."[7] That the truth content of a text lies not in the literal sense of the written word but in the dynamism between the word and the reader suggests or rather affirms what other scholars have said as regards the proper hermeneutical approach to any given discourse. Claude Levi-Strauss, for example, applying this hermeneutical principle in interpreting his theory of myth said that the unity of myth and its proper meaning "appears behind and beyond the text and, in the best hypothesis, will become a reality in the mind of the reader."[8] Again, the dynamics between the words or text and reader, brings out what Paul Ricoeur called the polarities of event vs. meaning, and sense vs. reference. According to Ricoeur, " . . . all discourse is produced as an event; as such, it is the counterpart of language understood as code or system . . . All discourse, we shall say, is realized as event but understood as meaning."[9] The connection between event and meaning as contained in a discourse brings about another polarity namely: sense and reference. What do we mean by sense and reference as it applies to discourse? It simply means, "Distinguishing between what is said by the sentence as a whole and by the words which compose it on the other hand, and that about which something is said on the other hand. To speak is to say something about something."[10] This affirms what Kukai said that the true meaning of text comes out in the dynamics between the words (which represent the authors view) and the reader (who applies his own his subjective understanding and interpretation to the text). As Ricoeur puts it, "The concept of meaning allows two interpretations which reflect the main dialectic between event and meaning. To mean is both what the speaker means, i.e., what he intends to say, and what the sentence means, i.e., what the conjunction between the identification function and the predicative function yield. Meaning, in other words, is both noetic and noematic."[11] This quotation from Ricoeur summarizes the dynamics that occur between the words or text and the reader, as a first hermeneutical principle in Kasulis' essay.

ii.) Understanding the author's background. Another hermeneutical principle in this essay is that for the reader to understand or interpret what the author said or intended to say, he must understand or at least be aware of the author's world view: his environment, background, psychological disposition, experience, culture, and if need be religion. As expressed by Kasulis, "In fact, Kukai himself emphasized [an] interpenetration of three mysteries or intimacies [in interpreting a text]: body, speech, and mind. To penetrate the meaning of his (author's) words, therefore, we must consider the psychological and physical environment in which he lived."[12]

The worldview of an author has a great influence on his thought pattern and method of writing. For example, an author who wrote during the medieval period, whether religious or not, cannot describe the universe outside the 'three storey idea' of heaven above, earth below, and hell beneath, whereas, a 21st century writer will express a more scientific worldview of the universe. To interpret the work of a medieval author, understanding his worldview is very necessary. This principle has a big influence on Kukai's hermeneutical theory. According to Kasulis, "There is a profound psychological insight in Kukai's approach. His theory suggests that a person's worldview is confirmed in his own experience. In short, one's mind resides in a world fitting one's own theory."[13]

iii.) A third hermeneutical principle is that the 'truth words' or the true meaning of words or text is seen in terms of what the words do or how they impact the reader or hearer and not in terms of what the words or texts are saying. In the words of Kasulis, from the writings of Kukai, "we find an early tendency on Kukai's part to interpret the meaning of a text in terms of what its words do as much as what they say or evoke . . . That is, a major criterion for evaluating a teaching is its effects on human beings who live according to it."[14] Kukai's major emphasis of interpreting the truth of a text is on the impact of the text, that is, what the words do, rather than what they say. Hence:

> If a set of expressions leads us to think about the spirituality at the foundation of ordinary experience and if, more importantly, it causes us to change our behavior and to undertake Shingon practice, those expressions are *true* in a macrocosmic as well as microcosmic sense. We could, therefore, make this definition of macrocosmic verbal truth into a hermeneutical criterion for interpreting and evaluating various religio-philosophical theories: the more a theory leads us to recognize the microcosmic and cosmic dimensions of reality, the more true the theory. This is, in fact, the criterion Kukai applied in a most creative aspect of his philosophical theory: his articulation of the ten states of mind. [15]

This is what I may call a moral interpretation of a text.

iv.) Romantic and Metaphoric principle. This is another principle that Kasulis noted in this essay. The meaning of text is sometimes portrayed in romantic and metaphorical language of poetry and art. According to Kasulis, "The work (Kukai's work *Aim of the Three Teachings*) displays Kukai's early use of imagination as a vehicle for expressing the dharma. To explain the teachings of Confucianism, Taoism, and

Buddhism, Kukai used an artistic device: creating a fictional discussion among proponents of the three life-styles . . . he continued to uphold the centrality of artistic expression, especially art and poetry, as ideal vehicles for conveying the most profound levels of religious truth."[16] This view is a very sound hermeneutical principle in understanding religious truth, because religious language is a language of romanticism, poetry, artistic expression, and metaphor. They are most often coded languages whose true meaning lie beyond the literary writings of the text.

v.) The truth of a text is found in the spiritual meaning of the text. The spiritual meaning of text, also known as the allegorical meaning, is very important, and in fact the highest level in the interpretation and understanding a religious text. In Shingon Buddhism, to realize the spiritual meaning of a text requires accessing the three mysteries. Accordingly:

> There are three mysteries or intimacies: that of physical gesture (*mudra*), that of meditative thought (*mandala*), and that of intonation or speech (mantra). For each intimacy, ritual supplies the spiritual context such that one becomes directly aware of the pure physical-mental-verbal *act* of Dainichi. In the linguistic realm, for example, Shingon ritual recognizes five seed mantras: *A, Va, Ra, Ha,* and *Kha*. By intoning these mantras (with the proper physical and mental posture), the practitioner becomes attuned to basic resonances constituting all languages. That is, through mantric

practice, one knows directly the "truth words" (*shingon*) inaudible to ordinary hearing. [17]

That is to say, it takes a spiritually minded person to understand the ultimate spiritual truth. This can be expressed as an achievement of enlightenment.

Application of Hermeneutical, Principles in Kasulis' Essay in Interpreting the Heart Sutra, *"Form Is Emptiness, Emptiness Is Form."*

The Heart Sutra, which, except for the mantras, is the shortest sutra, centers on the emptiness of all things. Our text for consideration is the teaching of the Bodhisattva Avalokitesvara to Sariputra. He said "Here, Sariputra, form is emptiness and the very emptiness is form; emptiness does not differ from form, form does not differ from emptiness; whatever is form, that is emptiness, whatever is emptiness, that is form, the same is true of feelings, perceptions, impulses and consciousness."[18]

How do we understand the truth of this sutra in the light of the hermeneutical principles contained in Kasulis' essay? Do we need to ignore what the text itself says, following the first principle in our essay that the true meaning of text is not in the letters written on the pages, but in the dynamics between the words and the reader? Again, can the reader truly understand the dynamics in the words without seeking to understand the intention or mind of the author, as revealed in the text itself? To all these questions, Kasulis, speaking for Kukai, would answer no. Even though the truth lies beyond the written words, nevertheless the written words or texts are indispensable in understanding the truth and in understanding the intention of the author. Accordingly, Kasulis said, "We cannot do without words. Kukai, a philosopher whose religious quest began with search for meaning in sacred texts, understood that point very well when he wrote: The dharma is beyond speech, but without speech, it cannot be revealed. Suchness transcends forms, but without forms it cannot be realized."[19]. Thus, in the view of Nagarjuna, we both need dharma and emptiness. Supporting this view, Sandra A. Wawrytko, a Buddhist hermeneutist said that in order to understand the true meaning of a text, "The investigator must begin with the basic text, the superficial verbal encoding of what the author did say. One's role here is to report accurately the actual words in which the message was originally encoded . . . A text is merely a written document, and so one must move to the next stage, decoding its underlying message, what the author intended to say. What is it that the words seek to convey?"[20]

Having explained the basis of the first principle in our essay, the meaning of the sutra, 'form is emptiness and emptiness is form,' is not in the nihilistic understanding of the text, which the written words may seen to portray, but in the understanding of the true nature of things as impermanence. The emptiness of all forms is not "nothingness, non-existence, or non-reality" but "No-Thing-ness." According to Dogen, **"Sunyata is not non-existence.** Sunyata is not the denial of real existence—**it expresses the absence of anything other than real existence."**[21]

Another hermeneutical principle in Kasulis' essay that we shall apply to the interpretation of the Heart Sutra on the emptiness of all forms is the third principle. This principle states that "truth words" or the true meaning of words or text is seen in terms of what the words do or how they impact the reader or hearer, and not in terms of what the words or texts are saying. To understand the true meaning of sutra under consideration, one should ask: what does the teaching on emptiness do the hearer? The answer to this question is that it helps the hearer to realize the impermanence of all things, and thus stop desire and attachment to things. This non attachment and extinguishing of desire will help to the break the cycle of samsara, achieve enlightenment and consequently Nirvana. We can see here that essence of the sutra is not to debate or argue whether things are empty or not, whether they exist or not. Such debate or argument comes from what the reader thinks the sutra is saying and not what the sutra does to the hearer. What the text does to the hearer is the moral meaning of a text in the theory of interpretation.

This brings us to another principle mentioned in our text, namely the spiritual understanding or truth of a text. In the case of the emptiness of form, the fully enlightened person sees things not in the physical or literal sense, but understands truly the emptiness of all things. In the state of Nirvana, which is the highest spiritual attainment, everything is one and empty. As stated in the Heart Sutra,

> All things are empty: Nothing is born, nothing dies, nothing is pure, nothing is stained, nothing increases and nothing decreases. So, in emptiness, there is no body, no feeling, no thought, no will, and no consciousness. There is nothing seen, nor heard, nor smelled, nor tasted, nor touched, nor imagined. There is no ignorance, and no end to ignorance. There is no old age and death, and no end to old age and death. There is no suffering, no cause of suffering, no end to suffering, no path to follow. There is no attainment of wisdom, and no wisdom to attain. The Bodhisattvas rely on the Perfection of Wisdom, and so with no delusions, they feel no fear, and have Nirvana here and now. All the Buddhas, past, present, and future, rely on the Perfection of Wisdom, and live in full enlightenment.[22]

The above quotation summarized the spiritual meaning essence of the sutra on the emptiness of all things.

Conclusion.

I must say that Kasulis' essay on the hermeneutical theory of Kukai is very insightful and revealing. Kukai's method of interpreting Japanese Buddhist Sutras and texts touches on the importance and the primacy of the moral and spiritual interpretation and understanding of a text as a means of realizing the "truth words" in the text. These principles, I believe is very important in approaching and interpreting the scriptures of every religious tradition, not just Shingon Japanese Buddhist sutras, but all Buddhist Sutras, the

Judeo-Christian Bible, the Hindu Vedas, the Confucius Analects, the Taoist Tao Te Ching, and the Islamic Quran. I completely agree with Kasulis and Kukai that

> "we could, therefore, make the definition of the macrocosmic verbal truth (truth realized through the moral interpretation of a text, i.e., what the texts do to the hearer and not merely what it saying; and truth realized through the spiritual meaning and interpretation of the text) into a hermeneutical criterion for interpreting and evaluating various religious-philosophical theories."[23]

Notes.

1. Donald S. Lopez, Jr. Ed., *Buddhist Hermeneutics.* (Delhi: Motilal Banarsidass Publishers, 1993), 1-2.
2. "Hermeneutics." *Encyclopedia Britannica Online,* http://www.search.eb.com/eb/article.9040159 (accessed March 4, 2008).
3. Edward Conze, trans., *The Heart Sutra in English. The Heart Sutra Online,* http://oaks.nvg/heart-sutra.html (accessed March 14, 2008).
4. Lopez, Buddhist Hermeneutics, 262.
5. Bukkyo Dendo Kyokai, *An Introduction to the Buddhist Canon.* (Japan: Kenkyusha Printing Co. 1984), 228.
6. Lopez, *Buddhist Hermeneutics,* 258.
7. Ibid., 270.
8. Claude Levi-Strauss, *The Raw and the Cooked: Introduction to a Science of mythology, vol.1* (New York: Harper & Row Publishers, 1969), 6.
9. Paul Ricoeur, *Hermeneutics and the Human Sciences.* (New York: Cambridge Univ. Press, 1981), 167.
10. Ibid.
11. Paul Ricoeur, *Interpretation Theory: Discourse and Surplus of Meaning.* (Forth Worth: Texas Christian Univ. Press, 1976), 12.
12. Lopez, *Buddhist Hermeneutics,* 258.

13. Ibid., 267.

14. Ibid., 260.

15. Ibid., 264.

16. Ibid., 260.

17. Ibid., 263.

18. Edward Conze, trans., *The Heart Sutra in English. The Heart Sutra Online*, http://oaks.nvg/heart-sutra.html (accessed March 14, 2008).

19. Ibid., 271.

20. Sandra A. Wawrytko, *Language and Logic in the Lotus Sutra: A Hermeneutical Exploration of Philosophical Underpinnings*, http://www.geocities.com/chris_holte/ Buddhism?LotusSutra . . . (accessed March, 14, 2008).

21. *Zen Master Dogen on "Existence,"* http://mind.CONTENT/ Dogen%20onExistence.htm (accessed March, 14, 2008).

22. The Heart Sutra, http://webspace.ship.edu/cgboer/ heartsutra.html. (accessed March, 14, 2008).

23. Lopez, *Buddhist Hermeneutics*, 264.

7.7 AN ESSAY ON "METAPHOR AND THE CENTRAL PROBLEM OF HERMENEUTICS" IN PAUL RICOEUR'S HERMEUTICS AND THE HUMAN SCIENCES.

Introduction.

Hermeneutics, which is generally, describe as the science and art of interpretation began primarily in Germany. Interest in Biblical studies and criticism was the basis of this branch of knowledge. The term "hermeneutical" was coined as early as 1737, and in the contempary period was developed by Martin Heidegger, the teacher of Paul Ricoeur. Ricoeur took off from Heidegger but made a big shift from Heidegger's concept as regards what the task and the central problem of hermeneutics is.

This essay deals with a critical analysis of what Ricoeur identifies as the central problem of hermeneutics: metaphor. What is metaphor within the hermeneutical circle, what is the connection between text and metaphor, what are the key issues raised by Ricoeur in this essay? These are some of the questions I will address in this essay. I will as well apply the hermeneutical questions and concerns raised in the essay to my personal and cultural background as a Christian, especially as it concerns the reading and interpretation of the Bible.

Polarities or Contrasts Raised By Ricoeur in his Essay.

This essay is full of polarities or contrasts which are indispensible within the hermeneutical circle. To properly summarize, analyze, and understand Ricoeur line of thought in this essay, one has to understand these polarities (which constantly kept occurring and reoccurring in the essay), and how they interplay and determine how correctly to read, understand and interpret a given text. These polarities and contrasts are: interpretation vs. explanation, text vs. metaphor, text vs. speech, work vs. word, event vs. meaning, sense vs. reference, speech vs. action in relation to the subject, reference to reality vs. reference to self, speaker vs. hearer, and spoken language vs. written language.

Ricoeur summarized these contrasts or polarities this way: "I shall list the basic polarities of discourse in the following condensed fashion: event and meaning singular identification and general predication, propositional act and illocutionary act, sense and reference, reference to reality, and reference to interlocutors."[1] How these polarities come into play within the hermeneutical circle will seen be as we summarize and analyze this essay, and as we apply the principles contained therein in reading, interpreting, and understanding a given text.

A Summary and an Analysis of Ricoeur's Essay.

In this essay, Paul Ricoeur assumes that interpretation, understood in two ways: its field of application and its epistemological specialty, is the basis or at least a prelude to central problem of hermeneutics. The problem of hermeneutics as it relates to the field of application is caused by the presence of texts as distinct from speech. Another problem deals with explanation as opposed to interpretation. Based on this understanding, Ricoeur formulated the central problem of hermeneutics as, "the status of written text versus spoken language, the status of interpretation versus explanation."[2]

What, then, is the relationship between the textual interpretation and understanding of literal work and the metaphorical interpretation and understanding of that same work? In response to this question, Ricoeur identified discourse as a common ground between the theory of text and metaphor. Text represents the work, while metaphor represents the word. Therefore, the difference between text and metaphor is simply the difference between work and word as contained in a given discourse. In dealing with a discourse, the hermeneutical problem will be to analyze the 'work' quality or content text) as distinct from the 'word' quality or content (metaphor). In discourse, which brings text and metaphor together, we come face to face with the hermeneutical polarity of event and meaning. According to Ricoeur, " . . . all discourse is produced as an event; as such, it is the counterpart of language understood as code or system . . . All discourse, we shall say, is realized as event but understood as meaning."[3]

The connection between event and meaning as contained in a discourse brings about another polarity namely: sense and reference. What do we mean by sense and reference as it applies to discourse? It simply means, "Distinguishing between what is said by the sentence as a whole and by the words which compose it on the other hand, and that about which something is said on the other hand. To speak is to say something about something."[4] There is an intrinsic relationship and an extrinsic contrast between what is said and what is referred to in what is said. The objective existence of what is referred to is subsumed in the subjective speech of the speaker or sense of the writer. Yet what is referred to stands or exists outside the speaker or writer, and do have or bear a lot of meaning distinct from the sense and the event of the speaker or writer. This new meaning is at times metaphorically understood and interpreted. This is what I may call a distinction between language and interpretation in a discourse. For example, a speaker says or writes: It was a **fine** day in the court today. The underlined and highlighted word fine, describes an event or events in the court today. But the meaning could and often be understood and interpreted different by people independent of the sense that the speaker or writer tend to make. Let us identified some hermeneutical issues in this example give above. The speaker described an event, situation, or something he/she noticed in the courtroom. The hearers or readers could understand the word FINE to mean it was a good day in terms of weather condition, it could also be understood as beautiful day in terms of the smooth and interesting proceedings in the court, and it could also mean that the judge imposed a *fine* in terms of financial penalties in almost all the cases that were determined in the court today. In all these instances, we notice a distinction between the sense made by the speaker and what the readers or hearers understood as being referred to. These also bring out a distinction between event as it happened and meaning of what happen at the event as understood and interpreted by different people.

The concept of reference in discourse, according to Ricoeur, has three nuances: 'I', 'You', and 'It'. These three correspond to the speaker, the person addressed, and thing referred to. In other words, hermeneutical questions as applied to any given discourse will always touch on these three reference points: who is making the reference, who is being referred to, and/or what is being referred to? These three nuances provide a very important key in dealing with the text, context, speaker, listener, and interpreter in a hermeneutical circle.

A metaphorical understanding and interpretation of a given discourse cause the problem of interpretation and understanding between the sense and reference, and event and meaning in a discourse. This is because metaphor is polysemy, i.e. it has more than one meaning – meanings that at times are not seen in the literal reading or interpretation of a discourse. What do we mean by metaphor in a hermeneutical sense?

According to Ricoeur, "Metaphor is one of the rhetorical figures, the one where resemblance serves as the reason for substituting a figurative word for a missing or absent literal word. It must be distinguished from other figures of style, such as metonymy, for example, where contiguity takes the place that resemblance occupies in metaphor."[5]

To understand a literary work, one needs to understanding the metaphor employed in that work. This is what Ricoeur called explanation. The question is: what does it mean to understand hermeneutically? According to Hans-Georg Gadamer, "First of all, as a hermeneutical task, understanding includes a reflective dimension from the very beginning. Understanding is not a mere act repeating the same thing. Rather, understanding is aware of the fact that it is indeed an act of repeating . . . it is a knowing of the known."[6] A total comprehension or understanding of what a text is saying is the key to unraveling the metaphor behind the text. This is what Ricoeur called interpretation. This is a sort of two-way traffic: from metaphor to text and from text back to metaphor. One cannot exist without the other in a hermeneutical circle. Expressed in another way, explanation leads to interpretation, and interpretation leads back to explanation.

The question that one would ask with Ricoeur is: does metaphor exist independently of the text? Ricoeur would say no, and rightly so. In Ricoeur's view, it is text that makes metaphor explicit. This explication of metaphor through the understanding of the text is what Ricoeur called interpretation. It should be noted that text within this context refers to written rather spoken language. Written text makes explicit what is hidden in a spoken language. Written text is futuristic in nature. Its meaning is not retrogressive but progressive. As Ricoeur puts it, "The meaning of a text lies not behind the text but in front of it . . . Texts speaks possible worlds and of possible ways of orienting oneself in these worlds."[7] Although it is the understanding of the text that makes the metaphorical meaning of a discourse explicit, metaphor and text (explanation and interpretation) are permanently intertwined within the hermeneutical circle. As explained by Ricoeur,

> The priority given to the interpretation of the text in this final stage of the analysis does not mean that the relation between the two is not reciprocal. The explanation of metaphor, as a local event in the text, contributes to the interpretation of the work as a whole.[8]

Application of Ricoeur's Essay to the Christian Background.

One of the central problems of hermeneutics as identified by Ricoeur in this essay is the relationship between the contrasting polarities in the process of explanation, interpretation, and understanding. Some of the polarities that raise much hermeneutical questions with regard to the Christian background are the relationships between text and metaphor, work and word, and event and meaning as they apply to the explanation, interpretation, and understanding of the actions and teachings of Christ as recorded in the Bible. The hermeneutical questions here are: what did Jesus say, at what events, and how are they understood and interpreted by different people and by different Christian denominations? Let us use the Eucharistic doctrine as an example. Narrating the institution of the Eucharist, as recorded in the Bible, the synoptic gospels stated that, "While they were eating, Jesus took bread, said a blessing and broke it, and gave it to his disciples saying, 'Take and eat; this is my body.' Then he took the cup and gave thanks, and passed it to them saying, 'Drink this, all of you, for this is my blood . . .'[8] The event of this passage is understood as the same by all Christians, that is, the last supper. Nevertheless, the meaning of the event raises a hermeneutical problem among Christians. The explanation, interpretation, and understanding of this text and event by Catholics differ from that of the Lutherans, Presbyterians, and Anglicans. Even among Protestants, the interpretation and understanding is not the same. While the Catholics accepts a literal interpretation and understanding of the text, some Protestants accept a metaphorical interpretation, some still a symbolic interpretation, and other a spiritual interpretation and understanding of the meaning of the text, word, and event of the institution of the Eucharist. For instance, in Catholic theology, "The Sacrament of the Holy Eucharist is the true Body and Blood of Jesus Christ, together with His Soul and Divinity, under the appearance of bread and wine."[9] On the contrary, reformers like Zwingli proposed a metaphorical and symbolic interpretation[10]; Calvin adopted a middle position between Luther and Zwingli by interpreting the text "this is my body" to mean a virtual presence of Christ in the Bread. Hence, there were no limits to the disputes in the 16th Century about the interpretation of the text, ranging from sign, symbol, and type to metaphor.[11]

Conclusion.

To end this essay, I must say that Ricoeur made an impressive condition in the field of hermeneutics. This essay shows an advance shift of the task of hermeneutics from the traditional approach of regional and general hermeneutics, epistemology and ontological into digging dip into the nature and composition of a discourse: text and metaphor, and the polarities that help in the proper explanation, interpretation and understanding of a literal work.

The questions I would like to raise are: Will there ever be a synthesis between the hermeneutical contrasts, e.g., event and meaning, and sense and reference, to produce one and same meaning in a discourse for all interpreters? Is there no possibility of reconciling text and context within a particular situation through advanced hermeneutical methods? Finally, what is the primary goal of hermeneutics; is it to bring out various meanings embodied in a discourse and leaves that to personal interpretation and understanding of every individual, or to foster a common understanding of the meaning of discourse? Philosophers of religion and scholars of hermeneutics should investigate and ponder on these questions.

Notes:
1. Paul Ricoeur, *Hermeneutics and the Human Sciences.* (New York: Cambridge University Press, 1981), 168.
2. Ibid., 165-166.
3. Ibid., 167.
4. Ibid.
5. Paul Ricoeur, *Interpretation Theory: Discourse and the Surplus of Meaning.* (Texas: Texas Christian University Press, 1976), 48.
6. Hans-Georg Gadamer, *Philosophical Hermeneutics.* (California: University of California Press, 1977), 45.
7. Paul Ricoeur, *Hermeneutics and the Human Sciences*, 177.
8. Matt. 26:26-28. Cf. Mk. 14: 22-24; Luke 22:19-20.
9. Francis Ripley, *This is the Faith.* (Illinois: Tan Books and Publishers, Inc, 2002), 246.
10. Raymond Moloney, *The Eucharist.* (Minnesota: The Liturgical Press, 1995), 155.
11. Catholic Encyclopedia: *The Real Presence of Christ in the Eucharist,* http://www.newadvent.org/cathen/05573a.htm (accessed January 31, 2008).

EVALUATION AND CONCLUSION

In today's contemporary society, no religion can claim isolation or has not come under the influence of another religion. In most cases, some religions today appear to be a hybrid of their original form. In the past, Hinduism and Buddhism were restricted to India and the Asian nations, Islam to the Arabian nations, with Christianity as a patrimony of the Western nations, and African

Traditional Religion synonymous with the tribal people of Africa. However, the religious landscape has changed. Every religion and religious people has something to learn from other religious faiths; they also have something to offer.

The essays in this work covered a wide range of religious topics from Hinduism, Buddhism, Christianity, Islam, African Traditional Religion, and Mytholgy to Philosopophy of Religion. These essays have revealed that Hinduism shares a lot in common with African Traditional Religion; Buddhism shares many things with Christianity, Islam and Christianity are like two brothers walking along the same road, while Hinduism relates in many aspects with African Traditional Religion. These similarities provide useful grounds for interfaith relationships and an opportunity to deepen one's understanding and appreciation of his or her religion. In the words of Raimon Panikar,

> The more we come to know the religions of the world, the more we are sensitive to the religiousness of our neighbor, all the more do we begin to surmise that in every one of us the other is somewhat implied, and vice versa, that the other is not so independent from us and is somehow touched by our own beliefs. We begin to realize that our neighbor's religion not only challenges and may even enrich our own, but that ultimately the very differences that separate us are somewhat pontentially within the world of my religious convictions. We begin at accept that the other religion may complement mine, and we may even entertain the idea that in some particular cases it may well supplement some of my beliefs, provided that my religiousness remains an undivided whole.1

The topics featured in this book have been treated comparatively and academically rather than from the doctrinal and practical dimensions. However, one question that comes to mind is this: can we reduce the practice and understanding of religion to a mere academic inquiry? The answer is no, because religious experience goes beyond academic ventures, it goes deeper into the personal and devotional life of the worshippers. An academic study of religion, good and laudable as it may be, touch the peripherials of religion, whereas the flavor and essence of religion is found in the religious life and experience of the adherents and worshippers.

Scholars of religion who do not practice any religion, or who study or investiage religions other than their own may have what can be called an outsider experience. This outsider experience is brought to bear on their academic study of religions. The outsider may have all the facts about the religion – the founder, doctrines, geographical origin and expansion – correct, but will not fully comprehend the heart of the religion, which lies in the devotional and life experience of the worshippers. So my treatment of the essays on religions other than Christianity in this work falls within the scope of an outsider experience, that is meant for an intectual purposes only and not as a basis for doctrine and practice.

.